Beauty Queen *Angel*

BETTY COMPTON

BALBOA.
PRESS
A DIVISION OF HAY HOUSE

Balboa Press books may be ordered through booksellers or by contacting:

Balboa Press
A Division of Hay House
1663 Liberty Drive
Bloomington, IN 47403
www.balboapress.com
1 (877) 407-4847

Because of the dynamic nature of the Internet, any web addresses or links contained in this book may have changed since publication and may no longer be valid. The views expressed in this work are solely those of the author and do not necessarily reflect the views of the publisher, and the publisher hereby disclaims any responsibility for them.

The author of this book does not dispense medical advice or prescribe the use of any technique as a form of treatment for physical, emotional, or medical problems without the advice of a physician, either directly or indirectly. The intent of the author is only to offer information of a general nature to help you in your quest for emotional and spiritual well-being. In the event you use any of the information in this book for yourself, which is your constitutional right, the author and the publisher assume no responsibility for your actions.

Any people depicted in stock imagery provided by Thinkstock are models, and such images are being used for illustrative purposes only.
Certain stock imagery © Thinkstock.

Print information available on the last page.

ISBN: 978-1-5043-7112-4 (sc)
ISBN: 978-1-5043-7113-1 (hc)
ISBN: 978-1-5043-7130-8 (e)

Library of Congress Control Number: 2016920270

Balboa Press rev. date: 12/20/2016

CONTENTS

Preface vii

Introduction ix

Chapter 1 Guardian Angel: The Escape 1

Chapter 2 The Car Wreck, 1968 10

Chapter 3 My Renter's Baby: Premonition 14

Chapter 4 Mind Reading 18

Chapter 5 The Early Years 26

Chapter 6 The Demon 32

Chapter 7 My Daddy: Demon or Angel 40

Chapter 8 Living in Fear 44

Chapter 9 The Guardian Spirit: A Crow 58

Chapter 10 My Near-Death Experience 72

Chapter 11 Bundle of Spirits: The Moment of Death 80

Chapter 12 Esther's Hospital Room 2001: Angel Escorts 83

Chapter 13 The School Bus Incident: The Shield 86

Chapter 14 My Sister-in-Law's Death: A Vision 91

Chapter 15 The Basketball Game: Spiritual Encounter 94

Chapter 16 Out-of-Body Experience 97

Chapter 17 The Beauty Queen: Angel Encounter................... 106

Chapter 18 The Celestial Sense 114

Chapter 19 My Later Years 126

About the Author.. 133

PREFACE

My spirit has soared to realms of greatness and fled demons of darkness. I have viewed miraculous sights, and touched heavenly beings.

Most of these episodes were experienced through two types of spiritual phenomenon. Some are from angel encounters, others happened when my spirit departed my body.

Most people will not witness this spiritual phenomenon during their lifetime.

To tell the entire story, I had to include some hurtful things about our family—things that I normally would not share with the public.

You will not see photos or drawings of celestial sights. Any perceived image would have lessened the truth of my book. It would be comparable to a stick drawing trying to portray a technicolor video. Impossible to do! You cannot simplify God or the angels. This is true for images as well as text.

Most of the people who would be shamed by this book are dead now. I can write the story without hurting the people involved. My daughters may still feel anxiety as I rekindle painful memories. I hope this book brings closure to some of the things they did not understand as young children.

When my children read this book, they may wonder what kind of DNA they inherited from their grandparents. I don't want to sugarcoat this, and claim there is no mental illness in our family. Just know that most families have the same problems.

I could not tell the story while Harvey's mother was alive! That precious lady would have been devastated. She didn't deserve to relive the horrors her son endured. Burying him before her own death was tragic. She deserved peace.

Most people want me to validate their faith. Can I say these experiences prove heaven is real? Did I see God and the angels?

Spiritual departures do provide some proof and assurance of heaven. But they do not compare to the proof we have in God's word. Even though I have seen angels, I still have to believe by faith. I am sure I have misconceptions about the celestial sights I viewed.

The difficult subjects of spirituality and mental illness are entwined in this story.

I am making an effort to tell my experiences exactly as they happened. The facts should speak for themselves.

I think it would be very easy to overstep the bounds of truth, especially when you start explaining what you witnessed as a spirit.

You experience it with a celestial sense. You are explaining it with human senses. Your powerful, celestial sense takes in vast amounts of knowledge, beauty, and love. Your human senses cannot realize this knowledge. It is impossible to remember all the grandeur you experienced as a spirit.

INTRODUCTION

I have always been a skeptic with anything that was supernatural! I believe there is a logical answer for everything. I don't believe fortune-tellers can see the future. They are just good at reading your body language. Ghosts and spirits are not real. They are only images cooked up from our fears and imaginations.

I have no faith in people who profess to seeing miracles, seeing angels, or saying that God speaks to them directly. You see, I believe God speaks to us through his word. We talk to him through prayer. How many times have I heard, "God is no respecter of persons"? He doesn't favor one of his children over another.

I've always believed angels were around us. I've read that they are often sent as messengers. Other than that, I never gave them very much thought. My main concept of an angel was the figurine that was placed on top of our Christmas tree each year.

I do not have a logical answer for the spiritual incidents I have witnessed. Before these strange experiences, I would have said, "There's no way, this is real."

Writing this book has brought back memories that I've kept

hidden for a long time. It's made me relive intense feelings and forgotten terrors!

These experiences happened during the most traumatic times of my life. That trauma is what's so hard to relive!

I've never told anyone my story—not my husband, my family, or my doctors.

The realization did not happen at one time. I've been searching for answers for thirty years. I couldn't decide what was real and what was a figment of my imagination.

Each experience brought me closer to an answer.

I also didn't want people to think I was some kind of fanatic! People would not feel secure around me if they knew all the strange things I have seen. They sure wouldn't trust me to teach their children.

I just put it out of my mind. I've been busy working and raising my family. I didn't want to complicate my life. Especially when I wasn't sure what I had seen or where it came from. Most of my life I have been in denial. I could not admit, even to myself, that these strange happenings were real.

Reading this book, you probably think my life was miserable. If this was all there was, it would be. This is not my whole life's story. I've had everything that is important—love, family, friends.

These brief instances have happened during a sixty-five-year span of time. They have only consumed minutes of my life. Have they made a big impact on me? Yes, but nothing like the impact my family, friends, church, and career made on my life.

I have encountered spirits. Some were angels; others were something other than angels. My own spirit has left my body numerous times. On a few occasions, I've possessed psychic abilities.

I do not consider myself a spiritual medium. I don't think I have received any special message through the angels. I am no oracle who can predict the future.

Strange things were happening to me. I did not realize they were angels until after I had a near-death experience.

I was in my early fifties. After almost dying, I acquired the ability to see angels—not in my head, but with my real human eyes. I also realized their presence in my past. I stood next to angels as they comforted me at different times of my life. I relived these experiences as if I were there, the first time it happened.

I've identified characters by past memories and feelings. If I call a spirit: angel or demon, that is what it looks most like to me.

I will share some of my theories at the end of the book. Yes, I said theories, because I am not one hundred percent sure of my explanations. These details show what I felt and what I believed was happening. There can be a difference in what I saw and what I perceived it to be.

I have experienced more than twenty major spiritual episodes.

Several were life threatening. Most were life changing. All of the episodes, made me realize, they were from a higher power than myself.

Sprinkled among the big episodes are many small incidents. Most are intuitions, vibes, or feelings. Seldom am I even aware they are happening. I often realize something that I was not aware of. Then I will ask myself, *"How did I know that?"*

The following chapters contain some of my most profound experiences.

CHAPTER 1

Guardian Angel: The Escape

I was born in Iuka, Mississippi. It is a small town located in the northeast corner of the state. Iuka is a Chickasaw Indian word. The town is known for its Indian heritage and mineral spring water.

In the fifties, downtown was the hub of activity. Many of my childhood days were spent playing in Mineral Springs Park, visiting the soda fountain in the drug store, and going to the theatre on Saturday afternoon.

When we ate at the cafe, I usually got a slug burger. My grandmother paid fifty cents for two slug burgers and a small bottled coke. After sixty years, eating slug burgers still rekindles warm feelings of security and love.

Some of my earliest memories are of playing on the porch of a big bungalow house. The lights from a car lot lit our front yard.

Dad worked at the Pan Am, our town's most popular gas station and garage. My family lived in the house with my grandmother for six years. The children in my family were all born in that house.

In 1955 my grandmother remarried. To my amazement, she

left me and moved in with her husband. I liked that man, until he took my Maw Annie away!

How could she leave me and move in with him? I was not the only one that missed my grandmother. Suddenly, my parents had four kids to care for alone. Their cook and full time babysitter was gone.

My grandmother sold the house in Iuka. Mom didn't want to keep it. We moved to Daddy's old home place in the Sardis community. A big house with a dog trot hall and a porch across the front, it was built out of unpainted wood. The house was located eleven miles out of town on a gravel road. Most of dad's family lived in the area.

Mom contributed the money she got out of her parents' house. Dad added the land he inherited. After tearing the old dwelling down, they built a new house on the farm. With a little help from Dad's brothers, they did all the work themselves. This young couple was so proud of their new home.

My mom got a job at a new shoe factory that had just opened in Iuka. She was one of the first women in my dad's family to work outside the home.

It really bothered him, because mom felt she had to support the family. Dad farmed and did odd jobs. He raised pine trees, cut firewood, raised cattle, and planted crops. Basically he made a living the same way his parents had.

The farm was also a wonderful place to live. I had cousins. Jack and Jim were just a year older than me. When they weren't busy doing things together, I got to tag along with them. They could fish, hunt, and swim. I helped with their chores and learned all about the animals.

Having an extended family was nice. We were with them,

almost every day. My aunts and uncles took us to church on Sunday and to town on Saturday. They helped us as much as they could. They realized their brother was neglecting his family.

Dad did not manage the farm well. His brothers were not rich, but they made a good living farming their land.

My dad had always been known as a hard worker. He was very talented in most of his endeavors. Since he was the baby of the family, he had more advantages than his brothers.

I guess mom knew the reason dad was changing. The man that worked hard to buy us things. The man that protected us, and took care of all of our needs. The man that loved us, and showed his love every day. That man was gradually disappearing.

My daddy had been drinking for about three years. It didn't help that we lived next door to the local bootlegger.

Our county was dry, which meant alcohol was not sold in stores or restaurants. If anyone wanted to drink beer, they had to drive across the state line to Tennessee or Alabama. Both states were only one county away and only a few miles from our town. Meanwhile a few bootleggers did a booming business. They supplied whiskey to the Mississippi dry counties.

Mom thought moving to the farm would get dad away from the whiskey, but it didn't!

Dad was gradually becoming an alcoholic. He started drinking more and working less. Drunken binges came pretty often. And with each one, he seemed to get more abusive. Several times he was so abusive, Mom had to leave him. We usually went next door to one of his brothers' houses.

He was the youngest of nine children, many of whom lived on neighboring farms. My daddy was the only bad egg of the family! His brothers and sisters were good Christian people. They would do anything they could, to help their brother. They would sober him up and help him to get in control of himself. Then we would come back home. Daddy would be so sorry. Life would be good for a while. Then it would happen again. It began happening more often.

I was six years old and in first grade at Pleasant Ridge School. School was out for the Christmas holidays. Our Christmas tree was up. Presents were under the tree.

Mom took us to a Christmas party at Genesco Shoe Company. Santa Claus was there. They had toys for all of the employees' children.

It was not just a little something. They had the best toys I had ever seen! I got a Tiny Tears Doll. It was the most popular doll that Christmas. She cried real tears. My sisters also got nice toys: a red wagon, dolls, an iron with its own ironing board. We got fruit baskets, candy, and a ham. It was the best Christmas ever!

We were so happy with the toys we received. Mom said, "Let's put them under the tree. You can play with them Christmas morning." There they sat. I'm sure they were the nicest toys under the tree.

Momma had been cooking Christmas cakes and a ham. The house smelled good, with aromas of cedar and sweets. My grandparents were coming!

I should have been excited because it was Christmas—but I wasn't. How could you care about Santa or toys when your whole world was crumbling around you?

I worried about adult problems. Going to school, meant I had to leave my baby brother and sisters with Dad. I worried about them every time I had to leave.

I remember the teacher asking, "What do you want for Christmas?"

I told her I wanted a doll because that's what most of the girls said. The things I wanted, Santa couldn't bring.

Problems robbed me of my childhood that entire year. My mind was never on childish things like playing, looking pretty, or making friends. That kind of stuff was so unimportant to me.

Daddy had been drinking for a couple of weeks. Holidays seemed to be the worst for him.

He came in that Christmas Eve in a rage. I don't remember what set him off. He started yelling, cursing, and pushing Momma around. He yanked the tablecloth, and spilled all of our Christmas dinner on the floor.

I had seen Daddy drunk before, but I had never seen him like this. He didn't look like the same man. His eyes were dark and full of rage.

We watched him take an axe and chop our Christmas tree and presents into pieces. The whole time he was doing this, he was screaming threats at us. He didn't stop until he chopped furniture, windows, anything he came to.

I don't know how long this rage lasted, but it seemed like a long time. He did calm down a little, and then he would be crazier than ever.

Next he turned on momma. We watched him slap her, and knock her to the floor. Both hands were full of hair. He yanked it out, when she tried to run.

There seemed to be no end to the beating she was getting! She didn't even try to fight back. She just tried to endure each blow and shield herself from the next one.

Then he threw her on the floor. He held her there by sitting on her. Bouncing up and down, he let all of his weight fall on her stomach.

Every scream Momma cried out, seemed to fuel his rage. She quit crying out. She may have passed out from the pain, or she may have lost her breath when he jumped on her. I just remember thinking she was dead.

Suddenly, he calmly stopped and sat there a while. It was as if he was straddling a log on the creek bank. Everything was silent. We thought the rage was over, because he got quiet. He stopped screaming profanity and threats.

In a few minutes, he took a cigarette out of his shirt pocket and lit it. Taking drags on the cigarette, he smoked until it was half gone. He made sure it was burning good. With the butt of one hand on momma's chin, her head was pulled back. With the other hand, he stuck the burning cigarette to momma's throat.

I'll never forget how she screamed. Every time I see a pack of Camel cigarettes, that scene flashes in my head.

I was the oldest of four children from ages one through six. We all watched Daddy hurt our mom that day. Three little girls pounded him with our fists. "Please, Daddy, don't hurt momma. Please— stop!"

Daddy usually turned his anger toward Mom. This time he turned on us. Roughly, he pushed us to the couch. He threw Mom down beside us. "If any of you move or say one word, I'll blow your brains out."

Daddy always kept a shotgun on a gun rack in the hall. He took the shotgun down and loaded it in front of us. As he touched the loaded gun to my head, he looked at my mom and said, "Run and I'll kill every one of them."

We sat there in silence for a long time—terrified! After a while he told us, "If you move off of this couch while I'm gone, I'll come back and kill you." He picked up the gun and walked out the door—going to get more whiskey, I'm sure. In a few moments, we heard his truck start up, and he drove away.

A voice told me, "Hurry. run and don't stop running until you get away. Run—now! Get up and go now!"

I looked at my mom, who was frozen with fear. I said, "Mom, we have to go!" She finally picked up my baby brother. I took my sisters' hands, and we ran out the back door. We didn't stop to pick up anything.

As we ran, we could hear Dad's truck going up and down the road. He was hunting us. We hid in ditches and stayed off the road. After walking a mile, we came to Mr. Kenan's barn.

From the barn, we watched as dad went from door to door looking for us. We didn't stop at my uncles' houses. We were afraid they would tell Daddy where we were. They would never believe their brother would hurt us like this.

Mom asked Mr. Kenan to take us to my grandmother's house. He didn't have enough gas to make the fifteen-mile trip. Back then, gas stations were closed on Sundays and at night. He siphoned gas out of his tractor to get enough to make the trip. Mom was fearful he wouldn't help us. Most people didn't want to get involved in family problems.

The Kenan's raised a large family. He was a farmer and a preacher. You could tell they were a godly couple. I guess they saw how desperate we were. They also saw the shape my mom was in. They assured us, "Pete will not hurt you in our house".

Mr. Kenan drove us to my grandmother's house. I think he was expecting daddy to stop the car. He put his shotgun in the trunk.

After we arrived, mom asked," How much do I owe you?" She

did not have any money, but my grandmother would pay him. He said, "You don't owe me anything. If my girls ever need help, I hope someone cares for them."

That wasn't the last we saw of my daddy. He was at my grandmother's house the next day. First he begged and pleaded for us to come home. When that did not work, he threatened us.

We never went back. After a few months, mom got a divorce. That did not keep him away.

That day, I heard a voice within myself speak up. It caused me to take charge and make my family flee. After all, I wasn't a child. I had been responsible for my brother and sisters for a year. I assumed it was natural for me to take control.

A six-year-old child did not have the ability to handle that situation. We only had a small window of time, that it was even possible to get away. How did I know the right time to leave? I feel sure my daddy would have killed us if we hadn't left, when we did. Of course, the thought of an angel never crossed my mind when I was six years old.

1957

My grandmother's house the week we left my daddy

CHAPTER 2

The Car Wreck, 1968

$\mathcal{M}$y second odd experience happened just after I got married. I was eighteen years old.

I got a job assembling telephones at a factory in Corinth, Mississippi. My second shift was from three to eleven o'clock at night.

Working those hours allowed me to go to college in the daytime. Three days a week I drove to school, and from there I drove to work. For several months, I drove home alone. I couldn't carpool because no one had my schedule.

My husband, Harvey worked the day shift at the local plastic factory.

He asked me to be extra cautious while driving home at night. "Always lock your doors. Never let anyone in the car with you. Don't speed." He also wanted me to watch for deer. They are bad to jump out in front of you at night.

I know he was concerned with my safety, but he also worried about his car. I was driving his pride and joy.

His first new car was a graduation present. He picked out just what he wanted; a 1966 Chevrolet Impala.

Even though it was precious to him, he chose to drive the old truck and let me drive the Impala.

The drive home was thirty minutes on a two-lane highway. I usually got home before midnight. Being cautious, I always did what Harvey said. I never drove over the speed limit, and I always locked my doors.

Then something strange happened.

Nothing stressful happened at school that day. My grades were good. I was getting enough sleep.

I had dinner with Harvey that night. He often picked me up during my lunch break. It was the only time we saw each other, since we were on different shifts.

At work, production was good. I chatted with my co-workers. Nothing out of the ordinary happened, until I clocked out.

I came out of the factory and got into my car. It was as if I were in a trance. I could not feel my feet touching the ground. Everything was in complete silence. I felt like I was watching myself in a dream.

As I drove out of the Corinth city limits, my foot pressed on the accelerator. I watched the speedometer climb sixty, seventy, eighty, ninety.

A white horse jumped a fence and ran across the road in front of me. At a high rate of speed my car collided with the horse.

The car came to an abrupt stop. There were no skid marks. The brakes were not touched.

When I hit the horse, it was thrown on the roof of my car. My windshield shattered. The top crumpled until it touched the top of the seats.

Harvey's car was totaled. It could not be repaired.

The car had a lot of damage to never leave the highway. I heard people saying, "How did she get out of that alive?"

I went to the hospital and had x-rays. I didn't have a scratch on me. The glass didn't cut me, and I didn't have a concussion.

I thought, *There's got to be something that didn't show up in the x-ray! I probably have a serious head injury! Maybe that caused my brain to play tricks on me.*

Maybe I just imagined I was driving crazy! Is it possible that this could have been a normal drive home until I hit the horse?

The doors on my car were not locked when the first responders got me out. I had not locked them before I left work, which was something I always did.

When someone called home to tell Harvey I was at the hospital, he wasn't there. My mom picked me up and took me to her house.

Harvey had been out drinking with some buddies. That was unusual. He liked to go fishing with his friends. He never left with them, without telling me where he was going and when he would be back.

It was hours before he finally found me.

I don't know if he was more hurt because he lost his car, or because he had not been there for me. He promised, "Doll, I will never do this again."

That was one promise he kept. We were married twenty-six years, and he never went out drinking with his buddies again.

I thought what happened to me was strange, but I didn't have a clue as to what caused it. I thought it had to be from the head injury.

I was so scared and traumatized by the wreck that I didn't think about what happened until weeks later.

Could I have been drugged? I could not think of anything that I drank or ate that gave anyone the opportunity to drug me. I had not taken any medicine.

This strange trance started, the exact moment I walked out of the factory. I do not think drugs could be that precise.

I never told anyone exactly what happened to me that day, not even Harvey.

CHAPTER 3

My Renter's Baby: Premonition

I have managed real estate since 1984. My husband was a home builder. He used his work crew to build or remodel rental property. That's how he kept his crew busy when the housing market was slack. Our rental property kept me in the business for thirty years.

During that time, I had a lot of experiences with renters. Most were good, some not so good. Some I would like to forget. I had one experience that I will never forget.

It was July. I rented an apartment to a young couple from Huntsville, Alabama. They came to our area to work on the Tennessee Tombigbee Waterway. The government was digging a canal to connect the Tennessee River and the Gulf of Mexico. It brought a lot of workers to our area. The husband, Joseph was a heavy machine operator. The girl, Pat was seven months pregnant. She was not working at the time.

They were living in one of my apartments when their baby was born. When the baby was about two weeks old, Pat stopped by my office to pay the rent. She brought her newborn son with her.

A porch separates my office and house. I was sitting in a swing when Pat handed the baby to me. She said, "Miss Betty, I want you to meet my new son."

When I took that baby in my arms, a vision flashed in my mind.

I saw Pat dressed in a short white nightgown. She was in the apartment, looking into the baby bed. She had a horrified look on her face. I could see her baby laying in a brown baby bed. He was dead.

That vision flashed in my head. It only lasted a few seconds. Although it was quick, it was the strongest and most intense feeling I have ever felt. Even when I've experienced my own grief, it wasn't that intense.

I almost threw up, I got so sick to my stomach. I not only saw what she saw, but I felt what she felt. Those feelings cut me like a knife.

I couldn't say a word for a minute or two. She was telling me she named her son Joe, after his dad, Joseph. When I finally got to where I could talk, I told her she had a beautiful son. Then I handed the baby back to her.

It seemed like she stayed forever. I was having trouble talking to her. Holding back the tears and concealing the pain, was so hard to do.

It was good that I had the rent receipt made out. I was so upset I could not have written a receipt. I just tore it out and handed it to her without saying a word. She was so happy to tell me about her baby. She didn't realize I couldn't even talk.

After she left, I cried for a long time before I could stop. I was hysterical.

That next day I went to work. I taught kindergarten at

Burnsville School. I told one of my co-workers, Mrs. Dotson, what I had seen. I asked her if she thought a person could have a dream while they were awake.

She told me, "When you looked at that baby, it probably brought back a memory of something you saw on television or read in a newspaper."

I didn't think about it anymore, because I thought she was probably right. I only had one memory of anything like this happening. My mom's neighbor had a baby that died suddenly. That had happened years earlier.

The next day a neighbor stopped by. He told me, "Your renter's baby died last night from SIDS (sudden infant death syndrome)."

I went to Pat's apartment to see if there was anything I could do to help. She asked me to come in. We walked into the baby's bedroom. There was the brown baby bed. Lying on the baby's rocking chair was a short white nightgown.

My Renter's Baby

CHAPTER 4

Mind Reading

his type of experience has only happened a few times in my life. I call it mind reading for lack of a better word. Although each episode was different, I knew another person's thoughts each time it happened.

Three strong episodes happened over a twenty-year span of time. Weaker episodes happened more often. Some were no more than a few quick images that flashed in my head. I never gave the weak flashes a second thought. The strong ones were so intense, they really upset me.

I considered some insights, simply to be intuition. If I had a strong feeling about something, I usually paid attention to it.

I am very lucky. I think it probably comes from the fact that I make more calculated guesses. There are times when I am more aware of details.

I never knew when it was going to happen. There was no way I could read a person's thoughts any time I wanted to. I did not do this of my own free will. It was something that happened unexpectedly.

The first time it happened, I thought I might be reading body language. A guy reminded me of my own husband. Could I be painting images in my mind of things that Harvey did? Was I missing him so much, that I was looking for him in others? Was my grief causing me to transfer memories of Harvey to another person?

Then it happened more than once. I could see images of things that other people did. They were more than visions, because I also felt their emotions. Their feelings were experienced over a lifetime. I was overwhelmed with a lifetime of emotions in a few seconds.

It was almost as if I became them!

I saw what they saw, but I also saw beyond them. I could also see things that happened in their past. They were not able to see this. I knew more about them than they knew about themselves.

Time was like an image on a video. I could back it up or speed it forward.

The Construction Worker

I had a renter come to my office. He was a construction worker who was in our area, working on a nuclear plant. He said he was a site foreman. He didn't want to stay with his men. He said, "I'm not going to be responsible for them when I'm not on the job."

A former renter sent him to me. I was about ten miles away from where his men were staying. When he came in, he held out his hand to shake mine. Everything was normal until I touched his hand. Immediately images started popping into my head.

It was like a movie camera that was recording short videos.

There was no warning or message in the images. It wasn't a premonition.

He was just doing normal things. I saw him driving a truck, kissing his wife, playing with kids, working on a construction site. I knew what he was thinking, and I saw what he was doing.

The woman I saw was a brunette with long hair. I felt the love he had for his family. She was his wife. I heard him say, "I love you, Jerry."

The images stopped when he let go of my hand. I knew all about him just from that touch. I knew he was a Democrat. I knew he liked fish. He wanted to fire one of the guys he worked with because he took some tools from the job. I knew more about him than he could ever have told me.

I just didn't know where it was coming from. Was it him, or was it things I knew about Harvey? My husband worked in construction and did some of the same things this man did. I had no idea what was happening to me.

I didn't ask him about his wife until the next month, when he came to pay the rent. I was so stunned. That had never happened before. I asked him if his family got to visit him very much. He said, "No, we have kids in school. My wife, Jerrica, stays with them most of the time." I thought, *Jerry—Jerrica. Maybe I did read his mind.*

Dinner at The Restaurant

The second episode of mind reading, was a very vivid experiences. None of the other experiences affected me the way this one did. This one happened several years after the first episode.

One evening I was coming out of a local restaurant. It was my favorite place to eat fish. This place held special memories for me. It was built on the exact spot as the house I was born in. I guess I felt like this restaurant was my old home place.

Chatting as I left, I met some old friends coming in. One of them hugged me. It was for no particular reason, other than he hadn't seen me in a while. His family had lived next to my mom for years. We grew up together.

Immediately my mind exploded with thoughts. It took me a minute to realize. *These thoughts are not mine! They belong to him.*

A rush of feelings overwhelmed me. Jealousy, love, envy, pride, and fear were some of the many emotions he had experienced. There were feelings that everybody has. The intensity of these feelings was greater for me than it was for him. I felt everything at the same time.

It literally made me sick. I gripped the back of a chair, until this weakness passed. It only lasted a few seconds. If it had lasted any longer, I would have gone to the emergency room.

My anxiety level shot up. Was this a heart attack? Breathing was difficult. It felt like someone was sitting on my chest. My throat was closing. I was going to faint. Fear gripped me. I asked myself, "Am I dying?"

My mind was on fire with so much activity, but my body seemed to be shutting down.

His thoughts, concerning me were varied. Some were not very flattering. If I wrote a book, I could not cover all the information I learned about him from that one little hug.

I was pondering, *what just happened?* As we drove home from dinner that night, Harvey asked me, "Are you okay? You sure have been quiet since we left the restaurant." I told him I had a headache.

After that, I was afraid to let anyone hug me. I shunned physical contact. I never shook hands. People probably thought I had a germ phobia.

A First Date

My friend worried about me because I had not dated since Harvey died. She fixed me up with one of her husband's buddies. He was a very nice guy, and so good-looking.

My daughter said, "You have a glow about you, that is just beautiful". "You must really like this guy". I think I was happy because I had such high hopes for this relationship.

We went to eat at a rustic, beach-style restaurant, located on the banks of the Tennessee River.

I was enjoying the date. The conversation was great. We had so many things in common. No one had given me this much attention in a long time.

Two wonderful hours passed before we left the restaurant. I had never got so close to anyone in such a short time. I was absolutely awe-struck by him. I could tell he liked me too.

As we walked down the steps at the exit, he offered me his arm. He was being a gentleman. Since I was wearing high heeled shoes, I was thankful for the support.

I slipped my hand around his arm.

Bam! A bolt of energy surged through my body. I was glad to be holding on to him. The energy was so powerful it could have knocked me to my knees.

That touch opened a window that flooded my mind with images, emotions, and knowledge. It continued until I removed my hand from his arm.

I knew more than I wanted to know about him. It halted his ability to impress me. It sabotaged the closeness we might have developed. I immediately saw and felt things about him that I was not comfortable knowing.

His opinion of me also changed. He did not leave the restaurant with the same person he came with. All the good vibes between us just disappeared.

My anxiety level was so high I could not hold the tears back. There I was, stuck in a car for a thirty- minute ride home. I did not want anyone to see me in this condition.

I was terrified of what could happen if he touched me again.

I can only imagine what he thought about me. I knew he did not understand the change in my personality.

I formed negative opinions of him. I had them, and they weren't going away. I didn't date him anymore.

An Intruder

A few times I have seen images of horrible things. Most of the time, they were just thoughts and not images of something that actually happened.

The next episode was different because I did not touch the person. I did not get an outpouring of information. I only knew what he was thinking at the time. It was more like a keen intuition, except for the fact that I saw several distinct images.

One afternoon a man came to my door. He asked if my husband was there. I told him, "No, Harvey's at work."

He said he wanted to talk to him about a job. I knew what he was thinking. He was looking around and feeling envious. It was nothing bad, until he looked at me. He wanted what Harvey had.

That included me! He wanted to take something that belonged to Harvey.

It was hard not to show my fear. He started looking around to see if I was alone. He tried to get me to come outside. My office was across the porch from my back door. He said, "Can you show me what you have for rent? Will you take down my information and give me a call?" I knew he would attack me if I came outside.

He carried a switchblade knife. An image of him kicking in the door popped in my head. One thought really terrorized me. He wanted to carve his initials in my naked body!

When I didn't come outside, he thought about grabbing the door handle. I quickly said, "Come back after four. I've got an emergency call." I slammed the door before he could open it. I went around locking doors and windows. I called Harvey and said, "Come home now." The man got in his car and drove out of my driveway.

I said, "Calm down. He probably won't come back. Maybe he just fantasized attacking me. Thinking about something does not mean he is actually going to do it." I tried to rationalize what I saw. He left didn't he, maybe he changed his mind.

That did not stop me from preparing for the worst. Sitting there in silence, I faced the kitchen door. I made sure my gun was loaded. The safety was off. If he kicked that door in, I was ready to stop him.

In a few minutes, I heard someone pull on the storm door handle. They didn't knock. I listened as they left the back door and walked to the front door. They pulled on that door without knocking or ringing the doorbell. I moved my aim to the front door.

About that time, Harvey's truck turned in the driveway.

Luckily, he wasn't working far away. He came home just a few minutes after I called him. I watched the same man who had been at my door earlier, run across the backyard. He had moved his car from my driveway. After he got out of sight, he parked on the side of the road and walked back to my house.

When Harvey got there, he wanted to know, "What's wrong?" I told him a man had scared me. I let the guy get away before I told Harvey he was trying to break in. If Harvey confronted him, he might use the knife he carried.

We called the law. After getting a description of the man and his car, the law put him on lookout. I don't think they thought I had a reason to be that scared. Speaking in a professional manner, they did not say what they thought.

I could not charge him with a crime. I couldn't tell the officers anything the man did wrong, except pull on my door handle.

My husband probably thought I was a paranoid little wimp. I am sure he thought I was imagining the danger. I couldn't tell him what really scared me. The next day, Harvey found a square hole cut in our screen door.

CHAPTER 5

The Early Years

*M*y married life with Harvey Compton started in 1967. *Cherished* is the word that best described my marriage. It is also the way I felt.

Before our wedding, I didn't trust anyone. Keeping everyone at a distance seemed to be less painful than forming close relationships. That didn't work with Harvey. The harder I pushed him away, the closer he came.

At first, I thought he was a spoiled brat that got anything he wanted. He was an only child. He wore nice clothes and had a lot more than I had.

The main thing that made me feel insecure was his close family. Their world revolved around him. They were not a wealthy family, but anything they had belonged to their son. I was not jealous of this kind of family closeness. I was just uncomfortable around them.

Harvey wanted me to be part of his family. He included me every chance he got. I didn't know how to talk to those people. I didn't feel like I was as good as they were. My social skills were very limited.

Harvey put me right in the middle of everything he did. His family overlooked all of my imperfections! I became the daughter they never had. A sense of belonging made me feel worthy of love. They showed me as much love and affection as anyone could. Belonging to their family was very precious to me.

I learned to accept love from people that were close to me. I had always built walls around myself. I trusted them enough to tear those walls down.

They wanted me to get an education, and they had the means to provide it. Going to college was never an option for me. I never even considered it. They supported me in everything I wanted to do.

Mr. Compton died in 1990. Mrs. Compton helped me raise my two daughters. They were in every extra-curricular activity that came along. She was always there to help. When her health failed in 2001, the girls and I took care of her until she died. She was the rock that supported our family. No one could have given any more to their family than she did.

I was wrong about Harvey. He was not a spoiled brat. I trusted and loved him completely. I had never seen the kind of love that he was capable of. He was definitely his mother's son! He not only loved me, he made me love myself.

We decided against premarital sex. Having the same belief about marriage and the home was the main reason. We didn't want anything to interfere with the commitment we made to each other.

Harvey felt responsible for me because I was so young. I was seventeen when we married. He was only two years older than me. I knew he cared about my spiritual well-being. He was the one who insisted we attend and bring up our children in the church. He would never ask me to do anything that was detrimental to my soul.

If we had waited a couple of years, our opinions about premarital sex may have changed. After all, we were teenagers in the '60s. The year we married, the hippie culture was a big influence in our country. The year 1967 was the summer of love in San Francisco. The Vietnam War started big in 1967, along with the draft. Even Tishomingo County, Mississippi was influenced by the times. Our lives were changing, faster than any other time in history.

Up until then, most students in Tishomingo County went to work after high school. Their goals were to get married and raise a family. Many didn't finish high school. They quit school and went to work. Very few went to college. It was not unusual to marry at age seventeen or eighteen. In 1968, three married students attended our school. I was one of them. Two of the husbands were in Vietnam.

You couldn't pick up a paper without reading something about drugs. Marijuana and LSD were the most popular. Up until that point, teenagers might drive across the state line and get a six pack of beer. That was the extent of their drug use.

It was the year the Vietnam War was put on TV. America was watching horrors of war that they had never seen before. It was also the first time we watched body bags being unloaded from planes daily. We felt the families' grief. All the tragedy and sorrow sickened many Americans with Vietnam. The world opened up to us. Our lives weren't contained in Tishomingo County, Mississippi, anymore.

Many went to college. If you were an eighteen-year-old

male and you dropped out, or didn't go, you got a draft ticket straight to Vietnam. There were a lot of protests against the war, especially on college campuses. At first we admired the protesters for standing up against the war.

All of that changed when Vietnam soldiers were disrespected for serving their country. Harvey cut his hair the day he watched a long-haired protester spit on a Vietnam soldier. That made us fighting mad. Most people in our area hated the war, but not the men who served. We knew what the soldiers had sacrificed. Everyone knew someone who didn't come back from Vietnam.

After one year of college, Harvey dropped out to go to work. He knew it would probably be the military. It was 1968, fighting was heavy, and the biggest draft started for his generation. Many of his friends were leaving, and he felt obligated to serve. Sure enough, he wasn't out a month when he got a draft notice.

The decision to go to Vietnam wasn't his. Harvey didn't pass the physical. He had a pinched nerve that affected his left leg. It was from an earlier swimming accident. He had mixed emotions. He felt it was his duty to fight for his country—a duty he was happy to serve. At the same time, he didn't fully support the war.

Harvey went to work. Our part-time jobs were not paying our bills. We lived on tuna fish and Ramen noodles. He didn't make the best grades, so he decided college was not for him. He insisted I stay in school. I would have quit and gone to work in a flash. I was so eager to be out on my own and have my own money. It was important for him to support himself. It was time he quit relying on his parents and (as he put it) become a man.

Even though times were stressful, we enjoyed each other so much. I had never been so carefree. For the first time in my life,

I was not responsible for anyone other than myself. I was free to dream and to follow those dreams.

With Harvey's encouragement, I got a master's degree in education and a broker's real estate license. I took drafting classes and learned to draw house plans. "You draw it and I'll build it," he would say. If I just mentioned something I wanted to accomplish, Harvey pushed me to strive for it.

He let me plan and decorate the houses he built. I wasn't very good at first, but I got better. He trusted my judgment. We were best friends, as well as husband and wife. If you saw Harvey, you usually saw Betty. We were partners in everything we did.

I was married to Harvey Compton for twenty-six years. I loved him with all my heart! I have never doubted his love for a second. I know he never doubted my love. I trusted him completely from the first day I met him. He proved his love daily by the way he treated me. That trust continued until he gave me a reason, to never trust him again.

We were married ten years before our first child was born. We didn't plan it that way. She just came along when the time was right. I think we were too busy to have a baby earlier. The whole time I went to college, I worked a full-time job. After I started teaching, Harvey's construction business was booming. It took both of us to manage that.

Our first child, Cortney, was born in 1976. Four years later, our second child, Casey, was born in 1980. Our family was complete. We had two beautiful girls. Everything was going great.

Betty and Harvey Compton
1968

CHAPTER 6

The Demon

The year was 1983. Harvey was a union carpenter. He had been sent to Aiken, South Carolina, to work on the Savannah River Plant.

Harvey had always been energetic, especially about his business! He loved working hard and taking on new ventures. I didn't suspect what was to come.

He was working ten hours a day, five days a week in Aiken. The round trip from South Carolina to Mississippi was twenty hours. He came home every weekend. No person could endure that physical stress.

The carpenters worked out of town several months each year. Normally Harvey took his camper trailer and stayed on the job. He usually took short jobs and stayed until they were finished.

Taking on more than he could do was an under-statement. He started construction on a house that he intended to sell. It wasn't unusual for him to build a house. He always built when he was not working on an out-of-town job.

Our business was not set up to turn a house over to a crew.

To get the job done, someone had to be there and be in charge. Harvey was not there. Money was wasted on labor, materials, and poor decisions. It wasn't the crew's fault. They just didn't have a leader.

Harvey had raised cattle since he was a teenager. Was I ever surprised, when he bought two expensive cattle farms. One farm was all he could handle. He didn't make any money on it. It was mostly a tax write-off. He loved watching the cattle, but he never had time to work on the farm.

Harvey had never bought anything without me knowing about it. We did all of our business together. He was totally out of control. He was taking chances with everything we had. We could have lost everything.

Just building a speculative house meant you had a lot of money tied up until it sold. He always kept back-up money to fund his ventures. Being a good businessman, he never operated in the red. Now he was running on borrowed money. He was spending on anything and everything.

In one week, he spent more than we made in a lifetime. In just two weeks, he practically destroyed our lives.

Unexpected bills started pouring in. I started getting calls about things that were falling apart. When he came home that weekend, I cornered him. He was avoiding me.

I noticed he was wound up. He couldn't be still. I wondered if he was taking those pills truck drivers take to stay awake. I had never known Harvey to take any drugs. He drank beer, but he wasn't even a heavy drinker.

He didn't sleep at all that night. The next day, I insisted he go to the doctor. We went, and the doctor prescribed a medicine that would help him relax. The doctor said, "He needs sleep. These pills will knock him out and let him get the rest he needs."

I don't even know what the doctor gave him. We were not familiar with any medicine back then.

It was Sunday, the day Harvey was supposed to go back to work. Our two daughters had gone to church with their grandparents. They went to their house after church, so Harvey could get some sleep.

He took his pills and went to bed. He asked me to lay down with him. As I snuggled next to him, I could hear his heart pounding in his chest.

After a while, he turned to me. I didn't recognize the man I was looking at. His eyes were hard, cold, and dark. There was no life in them. My Harvey was not there.

In a very gravelly voice he said, "You think you know me, but you don't." He was talking constantly, talking to dead people. He talked about what happened to David Compton when he died. David was a cousin of Harvey's who had died a year before. He hadn't seen him in years and was not close to him at all. He talked like he was there when David died.

He told me he was going to kill me. "This is the last day you're going to live."

I said, "No, I don't want to leave my girls."

"This is the last day Harvey is going to live, and you're going with him." A third person that did not claim to be Harvey was talking.

He dragged me out of bed and threw me into the window. The window shattered. It was a double-paned insulated window, which is the only thing that kept me from going through it. He lifted me over his head and used all his strength to throw me. He intended to kill me. He did not hold anything back. We were in an upstairs bedroom.

"Don't be afraid. It doesn't hurt to die! Fear of dying is worse than death. You are going to die today."

His rage seemed to come in waves. He would be really violent, shouting vile obscenities and threats. He would almost kill me, and then he would calm down a little. Talking never ceased. In a little while, the rage would come back.

He could have killed me at any time, but he was toying with me, saying and doing things that hurt me. This went on for two hours.

He had a super recall. Chapters and verses from the Bible were quoted as if he was reading them. Harvey had been raised in the church. I know he had heard a lot of sermons, but I don't think he could have remembered over two or three verses. Harvey was not one to talk religion. It was disgusting to hear the word of God coming from such a vile being.

The Bible knowledge was also a way of intimidating me. He tried to convince me that prayer and asking God for help was to no avail. He was in complete control of me.

Past events were described to the smallest detail. It was almost as if he had been there. He told me dates of things that happened early in his life.

Information about death really stood out. He described the death of his grandparents, a neighbor, and his dog. It was as if he was looking at a picture of what happened on the days they died.

He told this story about his first day of school.

"In 1952, I started to school at Holloway. Miss Betty Foote, a teacher at the school, stopped by my house. She was driving a black 1949 model Chevrolet. I was riding to school with her.

Mom walked me to her car. I got in her front seat. I wore my new school clothes—a blue plaid shirt with navy blue pants. I wanted to wear my cowboy suit, but Mom wouldn't let me."

His stories were full of details. The evil way he was communicating with me was not in his stories. I think the stories were clearly memories he was seeing. These detailed stories rolled out of his mouth with a greater fluency than most people use when reading.

Normally, Harvey couldn't even remember our anniversary. Forgotten memories seemed to be vividly renewed. He also talked about seeing people that were not alive during in his lifetime. He told me, "I talked to a stranger," who was really my grandmother.

Talking seemed to distract him from the worst violence. When he quit talking, he attacked me. I cannot even repeat some of the ways he hurt me that day. I try to block them out of my mind.

I could see that he was ready to end it. With a surge of strength, he dragged me into the bathroom. While the tub was filling, he picked me up and threw me in. It was not deep enough to drown me. I thought he was going to break my neck. Blood gushed from my lip and nose. Everything was black with twinkling lights. I was probably passing out when my head hit the bathtub. The water was still running. He was at his worst. I saw nothing of Harvey in those eyes.

I did not say this out loud. In my head, I called, "Daddy, please help me." I don't know why I called him. My daddy was the last person I would ask for help. He had never been there for me!

When he leaned over the bathtub and put his hands around my neck, I knew this was it! He was going to drown me. Suddenly, he jerked his head around and looked in the doorway. He reacted as if someone called him. He said, "Pete." Then he jumped up and left the bathroom.

I crawled out of the tub. Everything was strangely quiet. Not wanting to face him, I hid in a nearby closet. The quietness did not last long.

As I hunkered in the closet, I could hear him stomping down the hall. The demon was back. With a chair, he splintered the door. The whole time he was threatening me. "I'm going to chop you up and throw your body into Pickwick Lake. George is going to be wiping you tomorrow!" (George was the local undertaker.)

He dragged me downstairs to a wall telephone. The whole time he was raving, "You sold my land. You are going to get it back before I put a bullet in your head."

I was selling real estate at the time. I first started selling our own houses and land. Later I got my license and took other people's listings. I had closed out a land sale that week. The land belonged to a client.

He dragged me to a desk, where he was opening drawers. I knew he was looking for a pistol. We usually kept it there. When he couldn't find the pistol, He got a shotgun out of his gun cabinet. "You are going to call Jim Jackson and get that land back." Jim was the lawyer who usually handled our house sales. He let go of me, but he stuck that gun to my head.

Even though he was getting louder, I could see a little of Harvey coming back. He would stay calm a little longer, between the rages. He seemed to be offering me a way out, when he let me use the phone.

I told him, "I don't remember Jim's number." Back then you had to call the operator for information. When I got the operator on the line, I asked for Jim's number. Harvey started knocking windows out with the butt of that gun. He was turning over furniture! He emptied the kitchen cabinets by breaking the dishes on the floor. The whole time he was yelling threats about the different ways he was going to kill me. The operator heard him. She asked if I needed her to call the law. "Yes, yes."

When Harvey was destroying the house, he was hitting the house instead of me. At that point he was actually coming back. He knew I was asking for help. The good in Harvey was allowing me to escape.

The Two Spirits

There were two spirits present that day, an evil one and a good one. I know I would have been dead if the good one had not fought for me. I also know I would have been dead if the good in Harvey had not been so strong. The evil one was doing everything he could to destroy me. There were times that evil was in complete control. That's when I barely survived.

There was no visual proof that a demon or an angel were present that day. I did not see anything except physical sights. I only pictured what was there by Harvey's words and actions. Even after I had a near-death experience. I did not see or learn anymore about the spirits that I believed to be there.

I wondered if I had imagined a demon. Did I blame this hurt and hatred on a demon? It was possible for me to believe an evil being could turn on me. A demon could … do this. There's no way I could call the vile, evil being that hurt me Harvey! I could never believe the man I loved was capable of this.

I could hate this demon so many ways. It changed the man I

loved, my partner, and my confidant. The perfect life we had built together was stolen from me.

Previously, I had no real problems. I could not find the time to fit in all the wonderful things I got to do. Now, much of the joy of life was gone. I blamed all of my loss on this demon!

That hatred was actually stealing my soul. It was a long time before I could concentrate on the things I had, rather than the things I lost.

CHAPTER 7

My Daddy: Demon or Angel

I never thought of my daddy as being angel material. In fact, sometimes I thought he was Satan himself. I was quick to judge him. I hated him for what he had done to us. But I don't think I hated him any more than he hated himself.

After we left, Daddy terrorized us for years. He broke into our house more than once. There is still a gunshot in Mom's front door where she shot at the ground to scare him off. He tried to steal my younger brother and sister from school. He stalked us for three years. We would see his cigarette burning as he sat in our yard at night.

He finally quit coming to our house when Mom married my stepdad, James. Papa James became our real father. He loved us and took care of us. He treated us like we were his own children. Daddy still tried to intimidate us, but James made sure he didn't get many chances to do that.

I finally stood up to Daddy after I married. I was still only eighteen years old.

He came to my house one day. He asked if I would take him

to get some gas. His truck had run out of gasoline. I did, even though he was drinking and smelled like he had vomit all over his clothes. When we started down the highway, He grabbed the steering wheel and said, "I'm going to kill us both!"

Instead of begging him to stop, I stomped the gas pedal. He let go of the steering wheel and said, "Slow down!" He was suddenly sober. "You're going to kill us!"

I stopped the car. I thought, *I'm not six years old, and I'm not afraid of you. I will not let you hurt me again.* I didn't say what I thought. Why did I let him anger me so much? I got so angry, I could have actually killed both of us. I looked at that pathetic old drunk and I thought, *He can't hurt anyone but himself. He's lost everything he ever had to alcohol.* I looked at him and said, "Daddy, I forgive you!" He got out of the car, and he didn't say a word.

That was a stupid thing to do. I could have wrecked the car. At least I finally had the courage to stand up to him. But that was not the most important thing that happened that day.

After I stood up to him, I could actually forgive him. Forgiveness freed me of a lot of anger and hostility. This aggression had been building for years. At last I was at the point that I was not going to lash out and inflict pain. I could now stop reactions to the pain I felt. The life I had with Harvey is what allowed me to forgive my dad. Accepting love allows you to give love.

I've tried to think of some good memories of my dad. Surely my childhood wasn't all bad. Sadly, only one good memory comes to mind after I turned four years old.

Daddy took my cousin and I coon hunting. I was five years old, and my cousin Jackie was eight.

My uncles were big coon hunters. They raised and trained Blue tick hounds. We loaded one of their dogs in the truck and headed to yellow creek bottom. It was a cool, crisp fall night. There was a full October moon. Most of the night, we didn't even need flashlights. Everything looked so enchanting in the moonlight. We listened to the dog tree a coon. My daddy carried me on his shoulder through rough places. We followed the sound of the barking dog, until we spotted the coon in a tree. We did not try to catch the coon or shoot it. Feeling relieved, I thought that was what the guns were for. That was the one and only time I ever went coon hunting. It was wonderful because I did it with my dad.

I know a sinner can be forgiven. But forgiveness doesn't undo the damage that sin causes. It doesn't erase the hurt we feel every day. Alcohol had caused my daddy to lose his family, his self-worth, and his health. Its poison had spilled over into all of our lives.

After being in a drunken stupor for twenty years, he finally took control of himself!

I was twenty-six years old and pregnant with my first child when Daddy quit drinking. He came to the hospital to see my new daughter. Surprise! Surprise! He was sober.

Daddy struggled every day! Staying sober had to be the hardest thing he had ever done. He couldn't do this without help, but at last he was ready to accept help.

He rededicated his life to Christ and went to church regularly. His faith in God gave him the strength to fight. He went in a rehab program and stayed under a doctor's care. DTs and withdrawal symptoms nearly killed him. Alcoholics Anonymous met with him regularly. He was fighting the urge to drink any way he could.

We enjoyed him for about three years. He visited and spent time with his grandkids. He was one of the first in our county to build a pond that raised farm-fed catfish. That pond kept him busy. He let the grandkids fish, but no one else caught his fish! His grandkids got to know a nice man they called Papa Pete.

Then he slipped back to his old ways. The doctors told him he was going to die if he couldn't quit. They were right.

Although he stayed off of it for three years, he couldn't undo the damage the alcohol had caused. He lost all control. He literally drank himself to death. Foaming at the mouth, he strangled on his own vomit. When it went into his lungs, he had cardiac arrest.

When we looked in his garbage, there were two garbage barrels full of fifth whiskey bottles. He had been on a binge drunk for about four weeks. One month of drinking was all it took to kill him.

Could my daddy be an angel? At the time of his death I thought, *No.* I judged him by what he had said and done to me. I did forgive him for what he did to me. I didn't condemn him; I just didn't dwell on it. I felt like a burden had been lifted when he died. I loved him, and I hated him at the same time.

I never thought about my daddy's spiritual destination until Harvey had that manic episode. When I looked into Harvey's face, I saw the same evil I had seen in my daddy's face years earlier.

I called my daddy when Harvey was attacking me. Harvey responded to that call. He immediately jerked his head toward the door, instantly stopping the attack. He called my daddy's name, "Pete." Did Daddy stop him from killing me? I felt his presence in the bathroom that day. Why else would I call, "Daddy, help me?" Sensing a spirit was the first hint I had of a psychic ability. Sensing is all I did, I did not see any spirits that day.

What I felt was unusual. This was just something else that I could not explain.

CHAPTER 8

Living in Fear

*T*his was not the only manic attack Harvey had. It was the only one, in which an evil being was present.

When the first responders came, they took Harvey to the local hospital. I rode with an officer, who followed the ambulance to the emergency room.

Although Harvey was still paranoid, he was calming down. His eyes continued to dart and his speech was rapid. There was no resistance. He responded quickly and quietly to all directions. I heard someone say, "They gave him enough barbiturates to knock out a horse."

The hospital made the same mistake I made earlier that day. They gave him medicine that should make him sleep.

In a few minutes, the medicine started kicking in. It had the opposite effect. Instead of calming him down, it hyped him up.

They strapped him on a stretcher just in time. He was uncontrollable! It took all of the first responders to just keep him on the stretcher. The straps that held him down tore the skin around his wrist. Every vein and muscle in him was bulging. He strained so hard, his eyes were bleeding from broken blood vessels. Paranoia consumed him. He lost all self-control. Harvey was not vile or evil. There was no sign of the demon that possessed him earlier in the day. This was a scared-to-death version of himself. His screams echoed pure terror.

They loaded him into an ambulance. I didn't know if I would see him alive again. He couldn't live in this condition. I think the doctors were expecting a massive stroke. Harvey was admitted to the psychiatric unit at Baptist Memorial Hospital, Memphis, Tennessee.

This hospital saved his life. The doctors were familiar with this type of crisis. They immediately got him to a point where he was not in imminent danger. It was several weeks before he came out of the critical care unit. Most of that year was spent in the hospital.

It proved to be the roughest year of our life. We only survived because of strong support from family and friends.

Harvey was never the same after that first manic spell. There was damage from extreme trauma. He also had complications from the medicine he took. He lived for another ten years. Diagnosed as bipolar and manic depressive. He was in and out of psychiatric hospitals the rest of his life.

We went from one doctor to another. We never stopped looking for a treatment, that would help him. At first we thought he just needed to find the right medicine. Treatments were just trial- and- error. Nothing he tried was a constant improvement.

A five-gallon bucket would not hold all of the medicine he took that first year. He took lithium every day. He also took uppers to get him out of depression and downers to calm him down. Sometimes he was so high he could not sleep. Other times he was so low, he could not get out of bed. No medicine kept him on an even plane. Every drug had an exaggerated effect on him.

Halcion and a slew of other drugs, were taken daily, to make him sleep. One of the worst side-effects of Halcion was hallucinations.

One night, he put his fist through the bedroom window. He saw someone looking in the house. I had to rush him to the emergency room. I wrapped his arm in a sheet. Blood soaked through the sheet and was dripping on the floor. He cut an artery. It's a good thing we lived five minutes from the hospital.

Both of us were at the end of our rope. The situation was life threatening. I did not know what to do. The prescribed medicines were not working.

The next night brought another hallucination. In his mind, he was fighting an intruder that was attacking me. Every time I screamed, he went into a fighting frenzy.

He pounced on the intruder that was lying in the bed next to him. All four of my limbs were pinned down as he straddled my body. Since he couldn't use his fists, he pounded me in the face with his head. By wiggling off the edge of the bed, I broke the grip he had on me.

As I fell to the floor, he grabbed me with his teeth. That bite was so hard, his teeth pierced my skin. Like a flying ninja, he came off the bed, and landed on me.

The attack stopped abruptly. Harvey woke up.

I am lucky he woke up when he did, because he was about to finish me off. I could not have gotten away from him on the floor. If the attack continued for a few more seconds, he could have killed me.

Just as soon as I could get up, I ran to the bathroom and locked the door.

His voice was concerned and apologetic. "I'm so sorry! Open the door! Do I need to take you to the doctor? I'm going to call your sister to come and help you! I know you're scared of me, so I won't come in!" Harvey pleaded for a long time. I finally told him I was not hurt (even though I was). I told him, "Don't talk to me, and don't touch me." I slept on the bathroom floor that night.

When I came out the next morning, Harvey was gone. He went to his doctor. He told him about the hallucinations and the things he did. That was the last time he took Halcion. The doctor agreed to help him get his medicine regulated. He signed himself into a mental health hospital for three weeks.

I thought, *I am going to leave him. I can't live in this trauma!* I checked on a place to rent. I planned to be gone when he got out of the hospital.

He was also thinking about the problem. I know he was thinking about ending his life. That was not a decision he took lightly. He knew the consequences for taking your own life.

The doctors said, "Thoughts of suicide are not uncommon in his condition." He was never that depressed. He just couldn't stand the loss of self-control.

He never wanted to hurt the people he loved. I never saw Harvey angry, hostile, or scared of anyone. He never had a single psychotic thought. There was no blame toward others. He did nothing deranged or desperate enough to even hint at being mentally ill. This manic episode was not caused by something that was seething inside him.

He was losing all hope. I knew he didn't want to live in this condition. Although these hallucinations were probably caused by the drugs he was taking. He thought the demon was coming back.

Because he lost control for a few seconds, he was scared it was happening again. That's why he checked himself into the hospital.

After a month, Harvey came home. He was not on any medicine except lithium. He seemed to be in full control of himself.

I didn't leave him. I knew if I left, he would definitely end his life. It wouldn't be because he couldn't cope. He loved his life. It would be because he wouldn't live in this condition. If this was the only way to protect his loved ones, he was ready to end his life. I didn't want to turn my back on him when he was in this state of mind. I was living with him one day at a time.

I stayed prepared to leave. A bag was packed. I was ready to walk out at a moment's notice.

Precautions had to be taken, if I stayed. I moved to a separate bedroom. We stayed in the same house, but we didn't live together. I didn't trust him. I couldn't allow myself to be vulnerable.

How I longed for that sense of security I had always felt with Harvey. I wanted my partner back. After the biting attack, Harvey took safety measures. He set bottles of medicine on top of the refrigerator and in three bathrooms. If I saw signs of anxiety, I had medicine that would calm him down. He had tried it in the hospital, and he knew it would not have an opposite effect. He kept it available at all times.

At that time, we only had one phone in the house. Lines were expensive. Each line was like having a separate phone. Harvey had four phones installed. We had one in each bedroom. He posted the doctor's number by my phone. He also put the fire department's number on speed dial. They were the only emergency service we had back then.

Bolt latches were installed on all of the bedroom doors. At

night, I locked the girls' bedroom doors, as well as my own. He might get in, but he wasn't going to surprise me. It would take a while to open those doors.

He also insisted I learn to defend myself. I was to hide a loaded pistol. "Don't tell me where it's at. Stop me if you have to." I had never even shot a gun. He insisted that I learn to shoot a pistol. He asked a friend with military and law enforcement experience to help.

He told his friend I needed to be able to defend myself. He said, "She has had several confrontations with renters who were involved with drugs." I did have a few problems. Everyone who rents does. Harvey knew he was the one I needed to defend myself against.

He bought me a .38 pistol, just like the highway patrol used. He insisted I keep training until I could load my gun, draw from a holster, and hit a target. I went to a shooting range every Saturday to practice.

Learn to defend yourself.

Being able to use a gun gave me some self-confidence. It was just one of the ways I learned to defend myself. I worked out escape plans. I learned to be conscious of my surroundings and alert to possible perils.

I learned to be independent. He sure didn't want me to rely on him. In all things, I had to think for myself, at home and in the business. He was capable of doing more than he did. If I got into trouble, he came to my rescue, but not until he let me wrestle with it for a while.

I am so glad, I never had to shoot him. I am positive I would never have gotten over it if I had. There were times my anxiety level was high enough to pull that trigger.

Sometimes I envisioned the fairy tale "Beauty and the Beast." I killed a horrible beast that was attacking me. When I looked at the dead beast, I saw a prince. I had killed my one true love.

After the first attack, I was consumed with fear and rage. I was a ticking time bomb. The least thing would put me on the defensive. The way Harvey was reacting to medicine, with hallucinations, was scaring both of us. I might kill him before he killed me.

In my head, a voice delivered a vengeful message: "Fight back. Stop him any way you have to." That voice was screaming profanity and hatred. It revealed all the things I would like to do to him. After all, he deserved it.

Was I going to listen to this loud voice, or to the quiet voice that simply said, "Forgive him"? These soft little words were powerful. It takes a better person to forgive than to fight back. I did not know if I had a forgiving heart. It was my nature to fight back.

I didn't see what difference it made anyway. So what if I said,

"I forgive you"? That was not going to change the fact that my husband tried to kill me. Totally void of any love, he turned on me with a vengeance. I couldn't forget that.

It finally sunk in. Forgiveness is not just saying the words. When I was attacked, I built a wall of hatred and fear between me and Harvey. I built it to protect myself from all the hurt I felt. This wall replaced the love, compassion, and respect I felt for him. My heart was cold and hard. To forgive him, I had to melt this cold heart. I had to show love and compassion again.

He never asked for forgiveness. He did say he was sorry! He couldn't say he never meant to do it. He couldn't say he would never do it again. All he could say was, "I'm sorry."

That was his way of asking for forgiveness. "Please try to love me again. I know I don't deserve you, but I love you." I hoped that I could believe him one day. It was just not going to be today!

My heart was not right with God! I was so full of hatred, fear, and revenge that I couldn't change how I felt. Feeling this way made it impossible to repent. Forgiving Harvey and myself was an obstacle between me and God. If it had been something that happened and was over, I might have overcome it. There was no closure. The fear, mistrust, and resentment continued for ten years.

If I took Harvey's life, the demon would use me the same way he used Harvey. I would become his instrument of destruction. It would be harvesting the seeds of hatred and fear that it planted. It would destroy my entire family. There would be no healing after this.

I knew the second voice was not coming from my brain. Two little words, "Forgive him." That was too simple to be the answer to my problems. Could forgiveness get rid of this fear and rage?

I couldn't see that far ahead. I didn't have a plan, but I did have a place to begin.

After the first attack, I slept in a separate bedroom. For months I couldn't sleep in the same room with Harvey. When you can't love your attacker, sometimes you have to love the man you married or the father of your children. You have to disassociate your attacker from the man you love. I knew what I needed to do. I just could not follow through with it.

I did the only thing I could do—I prayed. Please give me the strength to forgive him. I can't say my prayers were answered overnight. It took a long time to forgive him. I worked on it every day. My burdens became lighter as I gradually released the rage. My fears became more manageable as I accepted God's strength and love. I had faith that I was not alone. I believed I would not be given more than I could bear. Sometimes that was the only thing that allowed me to close my eyes at night.

I did not want to learn to shoot a gun. I was scared of them. Could mastering a firearm give Harvey some assurance? Would he believe I was capable of defending myself? I hoped he would quit considering suicide as a solution for stopping the demon.

A gun would have been useless in the manic spells I experienced. They were too overpowering and unexpected. A gun cannot defend you from a demon. Still, it gave Harvey some peace to know that I could shoot it.

There were times that knowledge could have worked for evil. I was now capable of pulling that trigger in a split-second. What if I was scared or reacted badly to a situation?

After that first attack, I had a gun in the house at all times. Although I did not trust myself enough to keep it loaded, I always kept ammunition nearby.

I've never seen Harvey shoot a pistol. He hunted with a rifle and a shotgun when he was younger. Now he didn't want to know how to use a gun. He didn't want to know where they were located in the house. We didn't have guns in the gun cabinet or in drawers.

In the ten years that remained of Harvey's life, I never got a relaxed night's sleep. Although the demon only came that one time, I could never let my guard down. I was like a soldier on alert, especially since I had two daughters in the house. I never completely trusted him again! In fact, I didn't trust anyone. Harvey loved me with all of his heart and he turned on me. I knew anyone could.

Even though you forgive someone, that does not mean you trust them. I wanted to trust him. I loved him, and I forgave him. But I never trusted him again. That doubt was branded in me forever.

I have become very independent and self-reliant. Even though Harvey's been dead twenty years, I still suffer from battle fatigue.

Being independent did give me the courage to raise my girls by myself. It also helped me to be confident and self-reliant enough to run our business.

On the other hand, this independence has kept me from enjoying close relationships.

Harvey had a zest for life. He loved people. He loved working and building a business. He loved sharing new experiences and adventures with his family. The men who worked with him were very close. He was their brother as well as their employer.

The medicine he took dulled that vibrant personality. He lost a lot of self-confidence. He lost that zest for life. Working and making money was his creative outlet. It really hurt him when he had to quit working.

Sometimes you would think, *He's overcoming this.* There were days when he acted completely normal. Sometimes the good days lasted for months. The bad times always came back. He was never as dangerous or out of control as he was during that first attack. That first manic attack caused a lot of damage that he was not able to overcome.

He never had any ill will toward anyone. He never lost his great capacity to love and care about others. Until he died at age forty-six. His greatest joy was his two daughters and me.

He never lost his love of family.

The Letter

Harvey's manic attack was not my only source of fear. A few days after the first attack, I got a typed letter. It said, "You don't have to be afraid. I'll make sure he never hurts you again. If you want me to stop him, put 'YES' on an index card. Stick it under the flag of your mailbox. I will see it."

I was petrified! I was afraid someone was going to kill him! I put "No!" on cards and put them all over the mailbox.

I knew it was probably one of our friends. Our yard was full of people that day—the fire department, first responders, police, and our neighbors came. Harvey was like a wild animal. The house looked like a war zone! The windows were knocked out, and the inside was trashed! I was wet from head to toe. I wasn't wounded, but a bloody nose made me look like I was.

It had to be someone who saw me that day and felt sorry for me. These were good men! I can't believe someone was really capable of murder! They probably thought Harvey was on drugs. They didn't think much of drug abusers or wife beaters!

I knew they probably wouldn't murder him, even if I had said yes! The letter was probably a result of a pricked heart and a rash decision. Knowing that didn't keep me from fearing for his safety!

The public didn't know the circumstances. Harvey wasn't responsible for what he did. The public saw me as a victim and him as a monster! I worried about his safety until he died.

Please don't hurt him

CHAPTER 9

The Guardian Spirit: A Crow

About two years after the first manic spell, Harvey lost control again. It was the summer of 1986. We decided to take a vacation to Washington, DC. We always took the girls somewhere during the summer break from school.

Harvey seemed to be doing fine. He went to the doctor before we left. He had a blood test to check his lithium level. It was good, but the doctor changed his sleeping medicine. That should have been a red flag. It was not a good time to leave home. Other than a few problems regulating his medicine, Harvey had been his normal self.

We loaded our two girls and my mother-in-law and headed out. Our first stop was Gatlinburg, Tennessee. We stayed there two nights. The Smokey Mountains was one of our favorite vacation spots. We ate at the Old Mill Restaurant. At night we enjoyed a country music show and shopping. While Mrs. Compton slept, we ventured an early-morning horseback ride into the cool, foggy mountains. It was so beautiful. Harvey laughed and played with the girls. He even stole a kiss from me. Everything was perfect!

The next day he drove to Washington, DC. I noticed he was quiet. Normally five minutes wouldn't pass before he said something funny. He was always picking at the girls. Today he only talked when you asked him something. He seemed on edge. By the time we got to Washington, I could see a big change in his behavior.

We had intended to spend nine or ten days on our trip. Our plans were to spend a few days in Washington, DC, and drive through the Blue Ridge mountains on our way home. After one day of looking at monuments and museums, Harvey was ready to leave Washington. He didn't pretend to enjoy it. He was too impatient to walk through museums. He wanted to change our plans and go to Virginia Beach.

I should have been heading back to his doctor, but I didn't. I made sure he took his sleeping medicine. That and lithium were the only medicines he was taking. I thought he would be all right if he could relax and sleep. He only took the sleeping medicine when he needed it

I took over the driving. Driving on the interstates coming out of Washington, DC, made both of us nervous. He was used to driving in city traffic. Not me—I had never driven outside of Mississippi. Just riding with me put him on edge. He couldn't sit still. Doing nothing was harder than driving. His mood was accelerating by the hour.

I exited the interstate. I could not go any further. I had to call his doctor. We stopped at the Natural Bridge in Virginia, just to get off of that highway. We spent the night there. Back then, I didn't have a cell phone. I had to check into a motel before I could use the phone. He could not hear the conversation with his doctor. I didn't want to scare him. While Harvey and the girls were watching a laser light show, I slipped out and called his doctor.

I was afraid this new medicine was hyping him up instead of calming him down. The doctor did not make any changes. It was not a good idea to give him any new medicine, when he couldn't monitor him. We also didn't want to mix medicines. He had only been taking this a few days. The doctor said it may need to build up to have the full effect on him. He wanted me to continue the medicine another night. I was to call him in the morning to report Harvey's condition.

After eating and watching a laser light show, Harvey seemed more relaxed. Mrs. Compton, the girls, and I were all exhausted. I was used to letting him take most of the responsibility for planning and driving. I usually just took care of the girls.

We fell asleep immediately. Harvey seemed all right, but he was awake when we went to sleep, and he was awake when we woke up. I don't know how much sleep he got. I was too tired to watch him. He was calmer the next morning. I stayed in contact with his doctor. I called him when I could.

The next day, we drove on to Virginia Beach. We stayed in a nice beachfront motel. Harvey was not exactly himself, but he was not out of control. He played with the girls on the beach for a while. They counted sharks swimming off the coast. The game was to slap the others on the arm and yell, "Shark" if you were the first to spy one.

I enjoyed the warm sunshine from a beach lounger. Behind a pair of sunglasses, I closed my eyes and relaxed. I could feel the warm breeze blowing and hear the lull of the waves slapping the beach. The smell of suntan lotion triggered my imagination with islands of flowers and palm trees. Oh, I needed this! It was so soothing.

After a little while, I opened my eyes. The girls were quieter when Harvey wasn't playing with them. They were lying on the beach with their heels in the waves.

Harvey was not on the beach. I thought he was in the room. I checked the room, the lobby, and the restaurant, but he was not in our motel. I left the girls with their grandmother, who was staying in the next room. After hours of searching, I was ready to report him as a missing person.

I finally found him two motels down the beach. He was behind a waterfall at a fancy bar, the kind you swim up to. He had a big mixed drink and three empty glasses on his little water table. There was also a pack of cigarettes with half the pack smoked in an ashtray. That was odd because I'd never known of Harvey going to a bar. He wasn't a smoker, and the only alcohol he drank was a little beer.

He was drunk! He didn't act up. When he spied me, he just said, "Are you ready to go, doll?" as if I had been there the whole time. We came back to the room without talking. He fell on the bed and went to sleep. I was glad he was sleeping, but I worried because his medicine warned, *"Do not mix with alcohol."* I was exhausted. I had to sleep when he slept.

The next morning, he was up, showered, wearing clean clothes. He was sitting there looking out of our fourteenth-story room at the ocean. Not a word was mentioned about the night before.

I was so afraid he was going out on the balcony. He could feel himself slipping out of control. I didn't know what thoughts crossed his mind. He was feeling overwhelmed. That's why he drank the night before. He was trying to calm himself down.

Alcohol worked as a tranquilizer. Trouble was, it was just a temporary solution. It had side effects. It was very dangerous to mix alcohol with the medicine he took. It intensified his depression and suicidal thoughts.

I called his doctor in Memphis and told him how he was getting more agitated. He wasn't sleeping. He told me to double up on the sleeping medicine, so I gave him a second dose. We left Virginia Beach and headed to Norfolk, Virginia.

In a few minutes, he went crazy! He was agitated, scared, angry, and crying all at the same time. He yelled, "That car's going to hit you!" He stayed in that condition for a few more miles. I talked to him and tried to reassure him that we were safe.

When we entered a long tunnel that went under the water of Chesapeake Bay, he completely lost it. He was screaming that we were going to die. "The water's going to flood the tunnel. The walls are caving in." All these fears were real to him. The hallucinations were terrorizing him. He reacted as if something was about to kill him. It was that real to him.

Unexpectedly, he grabbed the steering wheel. I thought we were going to wreck! I said, "Harvey, you're scaring the girls." He let go of the steering wheel and looked at our daughters in the backseat.

After sitting still for just a few seconds, he grabbed the door handle. Escape was on his mind! The only thing that saved him is that it's hard to open a car door when you're going fifty mph. I saw the end of the tunnel, and I tried to calm him by telling him, "We're coming out of the water!" He quit trying to open the door.

After I left the tunnel, I saw my salvation—a sign with a blue letter H. It was a hospital sign. I immediately took the exit and turned into the drive of a hospital emergency room.

Hospital security tried to get Harvey out of the car. They were not successful with that effort. He locked the doors and hid behind the seats. I was afraid he was going to open the door and run away. If that happened, there would be no talking him back.

They called two law cars. I was scared to death. I knew he was going to fight them. They might shoot him if he attacked them. I knew they wouldn't allow Harvey to hurt them. I yelled, "He doesn't have a weapon! He doesn't know what he's doing."

The officers talked to him and gained his confidence. Thank goodness! Harvey didn't fight them. He held up his hands for the officers to handcuff him. When they got him into their car, they delivered him to the nearest psychiatric hospital.

After dropping Mrs. Compton and the girls off at the nearest motel, I spent hours getting him admitted. I couldn't see him for three weeks. The nurses kept me informed about his condition. I was scared to leave him in a strange place, but it was also a big relief. He was at the point that he was going to hurt himself or hurt his family.

At first, I didn't go home because I thought he would be ready to leave in a couple of days. I stayed close by, in case I was needed.

I worried if I was doing the right thing by admitting him for this type of treatment. Twenty years after his death, I still don't know if I did the right thing for Harvey.

I wanted to know what caused this behavior. How could I prevent it from ever happening again? The doctors didn't have a quick solution for me. His diagnosis was manic-depressive behavior. Long-term treatment was required. They said he would be on lithium the rest of his life. He also needed depressive and anti-depressive medicines to control his mood swings. He would have to be under a doctor's care at all times. He would need regular blood tests to monitor his lithium levels.

Our future looked bleak! Both times this happened to Harvey,

I didn't think he would live through it. The attack was so traumatic I didn't know if he could recover.

I didn't completely agree with the doctor's diagnosis, but I had to trust them to do what was best for Harvey. The only reason he agreed to psychiatric treatment after the first spell was to prevent it from ever happening again. He took medicine, even though it came with its own problems and dangerous side effects. Even though it was so damaging, he thought he had to have it to prevent a dangerous situation.

Well, it had happened a second time. This time he was on medicine. The treatment wasn't solving the problem he needed to solve.

I didn't have any other options. If he lost control a third time, someone might not live through it. Harvey was a danger to himself and to his family. Maybe this was the answer. I had to give psychiatric treatment a chance to work.

I tried to hide as much as I could from the girls. They were traumatized by the tunnel meltdown. Watching the law take their daddy away in handcuffs brought them to tears. I told them that he had not done anything wrong. They didn't take him to jail. He was in a hospital, and he would get better.

We stayed in Virginia most of the summer. I took the girls to Busch Gardens, the beach, Williamsburg, Jamestown, museums, and many historical sites. I hoped having a fun vacation would erase some of the hurt they felt. The girls learned a lot of history that summer. It was also nice to spend some carefree time with them.

Now for the part that involved a spirit. When I was in the tunnel, Harvey grabbed the steering wheel. The car should have wrecked. He didn't just touch it—he grabbed it and pulled it to him. The car should have veered to the right, but it didn't. It stayed on the road. Something kept it on the road.

The crow

In the mornings, I would sit on the balcony of our two-story motel and drink coffee. There were two huge trees on the grounds of the motel. They were covered in some kind of moss. Crows roosted in those trees at night. They were so big that I thought they might be ravens. The motel manager said they were crows. Each morning there would be eight or ten crows eating on the ground under the trees. After a couple of mornings, I noticed one crow sitting on a tree limb alone. The whole time I was drinking my coffee, that crow never left the tree to feed with the others. I felt like that bird was watching me.

Of course, I had Harvey on my mind. It had been weeks, and he was no better than he was when I first admitted him. I was so stressed that I actually felt nauseated most of the time. I couldn't let my two daughters know how I felt.

Every time I went on the balcony to drink coffee, I prayed. I did not know how to word a prayer for what I needed. One day, I quoted Philippians 4:13: "I can do all things through Christ, who strengthens me." I always ended it by praying for Harvey and our family. Each day I continued to use that verse in my prayers. I did not know why that verse popped into my head. It was not one I had memorized. I did not even know where it was located in the Bible. I paraphrased, "I know I can do this with God's help."

Each day my prayer was answered. I had the strength to get through that one day without giving in to the despair that was overwhelming me. I could not get through two days without praying. Each day it was, *"Ask* and *receive."* I learned I had to accept God's help. Even if you don't know what to say, all you have to do is ask. God knows what you need before you put it into words. He knows what you need, even if you can't put it into words

I was allowed to call the hospital and check on Harvey's

progress. I did that for three weeks. Then I got to visit him in a big room filled with tables. There were other patients there with their families. I was relieved when I saw him.

He wasn't agitated and fretful. At the same time, he didn't have that quick wit and friendly personality that was peculiar to my Harvey. He looked a little paranoid. He cut his eyes at each little surprise. I knew he didn't trust anyone in the room, including me.

Demon Possessed

At my second visit, I saw a black woman in her twenties sitting at a table. She had a visitor, but she wasn't talking very much. She had deep scratches around both eyes. Harvey told me her name was Jewel. He said, "Voices tell her to scratch out her eyeballs." The nurses tied her hands at night to protect her.

I saw and felt a dark being in her. I did not make eye contact. I didn't want that spirit to know I saw it. Since I was aware of its presence, did that make me more susceptible to its control? Rather than having a distinct shape, it molded itself to the shape of her body. There was no part of her body that it did not fill. This dark, volatile, angry energy was in control of the woman. Was she possessed by a demon?

Being aware of this evilness really upset me. Feelings of fear and loathing overcame me. I also felt powerless and completely intimidated. Could this thing reach me?

I thought, *Stress is driving me crazy. I'm imagining things. Am I hallucinating like Harvey? I may have schizophrenia. While researching Harvey's illness, I learned that people with this mental illness hear voices and see things that are not real.*

That was the first time I ever saw a dark spirit. I saw it with my eyes, the same way I saw the woman sitting next to it. I didn't dream it. I didn't know what to call it. Demon, devil, evil spirit—it had to be one of these things. Could this be what was inside Harvey when he had the manic attack?

It looked like what I imagined a demon to be, so that's what I called it. I was so shaken! I had never seen anything like this. I would have run away if I could. The doors to the hospital locked when I came in. Besides, the hospital might try to keep me if I told them what I saw.

There were only eight patients in this room. I looked around to see if I saw any more like her. I didn't. I thought, *what is Harvey locked up with?*

I slowly walked to the nurse's station. She was behind a glass door that had wire over it. I asked her to open the door and let me out. She said, "You have thirty minutes. You've only been here ten minutes." She didn't say any more when I said, "Let me out, now!"

I walked out of the hospital. When I got outside, tears were rolling down my cheek. I started walking around the grounds. It looked like a park with sidewalks that were lined with flower and trees. I kept walking because I couldn't quit crying. I had to calm down! I couldn't see to drive because of the tears. I made three long laps around the hospital grounds before I went to my car.

I saw Harvey three times a week. Each visit lasted for one hour. He was not glad to see me. I think he was relieved when I left. For the first time in our time together, I did not see any love for me. There wasn't any hate, and I don't think he wished me any harm. He just seemed more comfortable around the other patients. I was actually a little jealous of Jewel. She was the subject of most of our conversations.

I was hurt because he didn't seem concerned about me or our

daughters. He never even asked about them. They had always been Daddy's girls! This attitude went on for two weeks. Was the love he had for us completely erased? Was this the end of our marriage?

The week before I left, I was on the balcony having my coffee. That same big black crow was on a limb about ten feet from me. It was looking at me. Its eyes looked like dark puddles.

All at once I had tunnel vision. I was looking through a tornado of swirling, bright light. It started out as small, at my eye, and enlarged until it was the size of a standing man. Visions flashed in the crow's eyes. Voiceless narrations of the visions were echoing in my head.

I saw the bird on the hospital sign. It was guiding me to the hospital. The bird was at the hospital parking lot. It was with Harvey when the law handcuffed him. I saw the bird at the psychiatric hospital outside of Harvey's window. It was on the grounds, watching me as I walked. I realized the bird had been with me since the first day, when I drove out of the tunnel. This was no ordinary bird. It was a guardian spirit!

I also saw a picture of the steering wheel when Harvey grabbed it. A hand held it and didn't let it turn. The hand looked like a normal man's hand. It was attached to an arm that was covered with a buckskin sleeve. The buckskin had wrinkles on it with rubbed spots that shined.

An Indian man emerged from the bird. From a dot, he grew to the height of a six-foot man. He was an older man with the kindest eyes. Even though an Indian coming from a bird's eye seems like a cartoon, this Indian was very real. He looked like a normal man. This area had once been his home.

I noticed things about him that I wouldn't notice about every person I met. I felt his breath, the texture of his skin, and his thoughts. He was dressed in very simple animal skin clothing, without any kind of decorations. It was sewed together with the tendons of a deer. He was a very wise and powerful spirit. Black paint was smeared across his nose and cheek. I wondered if it was war paint. If it was, I knew he didn't mean me any harm.

A messenger had been sent to help me. He brought me strength, peace, and understanding. Not only me, he was also there for Harvey. The Indian disappeared back into the bird's eye. Without saying a single word, he gave me everything I needed. He was the answer to my prayers. The bird flew away. His job was finished. I didn't see the bird or the Indian again.

This was the day Harvey was being discharged from the hospital. Earlier that week, I was working myself into a nervous frenzy. I dreaded the ten-hour trip home. My hospital visits hadn't convinced me that he was ready to be discharged. He was heavily medicated. I didn't know what could happen when his medicine was not being monitored. I remembered how drugs took away all of Harvey's self-control.

Terrified and paranoid seemed to describe me the best. I was not going to bring the same man home that I admitted to that hospital. I just could not do it. Even though I wanted Harvey to come home, I was not ready to face him. Was I going to panic and run away? I was on the verge of running! I wanted to escape and never look back.

The Indian I saw was an angel. Seeing the angel changed me. A sense of complete serenity came over me. That night, I slept better than I had in months. A strong, calm, confident person walked into that hospital on discharge day.

My fears were not going to overwhelm me. I had confidence in my ability to make the right decisions for Harvey and for my girls. What I had to do was going to be done. I knew I would have help doing it!

Harvey was dismissed. After eight weeks, we finally left Virginia.

I didn't have time to think about what I saw and felt before Harvey's dismissal. On the way home, I relived the angel visits. As usual, I doubted my sanity. I thought, *that tunnel of light must have been me passing out. Did I imagine those visions! Was I dreaming? Is this a mental illness?*

I was standing the whole time. If I had passed out, I would have fallen. When I've passed out before, I went into a dark tunnel. I drifted from a large area to a small area inside the tunnel.

This experience was a swirling tunnel of bright lights that went from a small area to a large area. I emerged from it, rather than into it. It was opposite to the spiritual episodes I had previously experienced.

I explained the first few odd experiences as being caused by some kind of physical condition. Now I was beginning to believe I was seeing angels.

Every time I see the blue H hospital sign, I look to see if a crow is perched on it. I've never seen a crow or any other bird perched on a road sign.

CHAPTER 10

My Near-Death Experience

*U*sually I just say I've had a stroke when people ask, "What happened to you?"

The truth is, I don't really know, and it takes too long to explain the details. Besides, people look at me like I'm crazy, when I mention I died or I left my body.

I've had bronchitis for forty years. Usually it only occurs a couple times a year, but it keeps coming back.

During four particularly bad cases of bronchitis, my spirit has left my body. These spiritual departures seem to be linked to this lung condition.

Yes, I rise up and look down at myself. It's as if I was looking into a big mirror that shows my complete body and a big area all around me. Looking into your own face is an eerie perception.

No, I've never taken mind-altering drugs. Although I feel like I'm on a trip, it is not drug induced. One of my out-of-body experiences took me to death's door. That's why I call it a near-death experience. I literally died.

I was in my bed at about nine o'clock at night. My chest was tight. I thought, *I need to get up and rub myself with Vick's Vapor Rub.* All of a sudden, I left my body and floated up to the ceiling. I saw myself lying on the bed below.

Oh no, it's happening again!

The first two times this happened to me, it didn't last very long. I thought I either dreamed it or it was all in my imagination. I didn't tell anyone about it. I wasn't sure it had really happened.

This time was different. I not only left my body, but I left my house, and I think I left this world. I moved like a spirit, but I still looked like myself.

I went through the roof of my house and out into the night air. Silently I drifted just above the treetops. Everything looked the same in my yard, except everything was more vivid. I was looking down on the treetops shining in the moonlight. There was my deck, and I could see the high point of the barn roof in my backyard. There was a piece of tin curled up on the barn roof. Dampness in the night air kissed my cheek. My senses were super keen.

When I came outside, it was dark. I quickly left the darkness and went to the most wonderful bright light. Everything had a scent. I knew how the textures on the trees felt without touching them.

Oh what beautiful colors I saw. Everything emitted this bright, beautiful, glowing light. It was the fall of the year. The veins in the leaves were all unique. I knew where everything was without looking at it. I even knew where the insects and worms were working in the soil.

Even though I sensed everything at the same time, there was no noise, or chaos. Everything was peaceful, calm, and in order. Sounds were soothing, like chimes.

I must have covered a long distance in a short time. I didn't feel any motion, and nothing flew by. I left Burnsville and traveled north, just above the treetops. I think I sensed more than I saw.

People were doing normal, everyday things. The landscape looked normal. I saw cities and farms, rivers and lakes. I also sensed what was written on signs and advertisements. I read that I was in Tennessee, Kentucky, and then Ohio.

Although places looked natural, they also looked too beautiful to belong to the world I lived in. The beauty came from the brightness.

I stopped when I reached a two-story white house in Ohio. Is this was my destination? I thought I was on my way to heaven. *Well, maybe not.* Silently I drifted, in a standing position, over the street and up to the front door.

I was using all of my senses at the same time. I could see, hear, taste, smell, and feel everything around me. I possessed senses I do not even know how to identify. They did not belong to my human body.

Softly and silently, I landed on a metal deck on the upper floor. It was bigger than a fire escape. There I was, facing an aluminum sliding glass door that opened to the deck. Although I did not hear a voice, someone was telling me to come in.

I walked into a room that was decorated like the 1970s. Orange shag carpet was on the floor, the wallpaper had little gold flour-de-leis, and a picture of a Spanish conquistador with a brown helmet hung over the sofa. The floor was four-inch planks with mahogany stain. It was eighty years old. There were six coats of paint on the floor. A single light bulb in the ceiling lit the room. I could see everything in the house without going into the different rooms. A calendar hung on the wall in the kitchen. The page was turned to October 1972.

There on a Hollywood bed, with a bookshelf headboard, lay my *husband*. My husband, *Harvey Compton*, who had been dead for five years. I was so shocked, I couldn't move.

Yeah, yeah, I must finally be dreaming! You see, I had tried to dream about him since he died. Sometimes I cried myself to sleep looking at his picture. I wanted to relive memories of him, but I never could. I was afraid I was going to forget him, because I could never see him in my dreams.

Harvey was lying on the bed in his favorite sleeping clothes. He wore a white T-shirt and a pair of white briefs. "Doll, don't be afraid." He reached out to me.

He looked real. All the little details I remembered about him were there. On his thumb was a small scar. He got that when he was running a trotline and caught a hook in his finger. There were the little peaks in his eyebrows and the dimple in his earlobe.

I could literally count the hairs on his head. His hair was auburn, but now I saw that he had three distinct colors of hair: black, blond, and bright red. I knew he had more black hairs than red and blond combined. I could see the muscles and veins in his arms. He didn't look like a spirit. He looked like my Harvey.

Yet, he was different. That wonderful, glowing light that I had seen all around me shone from him. The serene, peaceful look on his face was not an expression that I had ever seen.

"Are you an angel?" I knew he was before I asked, "You'll know everything when it's time." He never moved his lips to speak. I knew his thoughts, and he knew mine. I heard no voices. All sounds were soft, soothing, and melodious. It sounded like music, but I heard no instruments.

He held out his hand for me to come to him. I was a little hesitant about touching him. I thought he might shock me or something worse! Whatever happened to me, I had to touch him. I had to see if he felt real.

I sat next to him on the bed and leaned my head against his shoulder. This was my favorite place to be—sitting by his side. We often sat this way while watching TV, or swinging on the porch.

When my head touched his arm, lightning struck! Something wonderful happened. It was as if all the cares of my life were taken away. My eyes had been closed, and now they were open. A door to immeasurable knowledge was revealed. I was aware of earthly, spiritual, and heavenly things. I knew the smallest details and the largest universal concepts.

I felt God's love! Love was in the light. This light was from God. I knew so much about God and mankind. There was no hurt or malice. Everything was beauty and bliss. Peace, love, and order was in everything around me. Everything contained the light.

"Am I dead? Did you come to get me? Do I have to go back?" I knew the answers to all my questions.

I also knew Harvey shielded me from the full power of the radiated light. I could not go back to my body if I felt its full strength. It was not time for me to die. He let me take in only what my human body could stand.

Gently he moved my head from his shoulder. In a flash, Harvey was gone!

I was on the ceiling of my bedroom, looking down at my body. I was repulsed by that body. It looked like a cold, sterile cage for my warm, beautiful spirit. Reluctantly I entered my body

If I had been given a choice, I would not have come back. There's no way I would leave that heavenly bliss.

I opened my eyes and called my mother. "Take me to the hospital. I think I'm dying!" I did not tell the nurses what happened to me. They would send me to the psychiatric ward. I told them I passed out.

My body seemed to be in shock. Every time my spirit has left my body, it has caused physical damage.

My doctor admitted me to the hospital within an hour of the near-death experience. They treated me for bronchitis. Extreme weakness paralyzed my body. My limbs would not move without help. I just lay in the hospital bed with my eyes closed. It took an effort to breathe.

My body felt like it was dying. This feeling started in my toes and crept up to my chest. I expected every breath to be my last one. It was weeks before I got my strength back.

At the time I was in contact with the angel, I was healed of every pain and care. As I pulled away, all the hurts and feelings came back.

This is all I remember about the near- death experience. I feel there is so much more that I cannot recall.

Psychic Abilities

This near-death experience was the beginning of many psychic abilities. I am hesitant to use that word as a description of the things that happened to me.

The dictionary gives the definition as; phenomenon that is inexplicable by natural laws.

Premonitions, mind reading, angel encounters, traveling to the past, and visions cannot be explained by the laws of nature.

I have always considered any communication with spirits to be supernatural. I never associated these with angels. Comparing anything that involves God to the supernatural was offensive to me.

I don't know where all people with these abilities get their powers. Some claim to be born with them. Some have more than others.

I only experienced small amounts for brief periods of time. The source of my psychic abilities was angels. Every source may not be the same as mine.

Abilities that come from the angels are not supernatural at all. All the angels possess them. Psychic humans only have a smidgen of what the angels possess huge amounts of.

Rising above the roof

CHAPTER 11

Bundle of Spirits: The Moment of Death

*T*hat near-death experience made it possible for me to receive energy from different kinds of spirits. This episode is the first of what I imagined to be dark energy.

One bright, sunny day, I was driving along Highway 25. It is a road that runs south of our town. I was going to visit my sister. She called and said, "I cooked lunch for you."

I was in a good mood. I really enjoyed our time together. We often walked through her garden. I was eager to see the spring flowers that were in full bloom.

At a certain place on the road, I was suddenly filled with a sense of foreboding. I felt spiritual energy. This energy was stronger than any I had ever encountered.

It felt dark. Light and dark are descriptions you use with sight. I call it dark energy because it emits sadness, despair, pain, grief, and terror.

I had sensed dark spirits before, but I had never seen one. This time, it was more than just realizing a spiritual presence was near. I was overwhelmed by it!

It did not feel vile and evil. I don't think it meant me any harm. There was no malice in it.

I sensed several tangled spirits. They were separate, yet together they formed a large entity.

It could have been a place rather than one large bundle of spirits—a place full of despair and death. The spirits were not angels, but they did not seem to be demons either. The dark energy covered an area as big as a room. Was this a door to some kind of spiritual place?

I started picking up little flicks of energy. The blue lights shot out like fireworks. It was not the soothing, bright light that came from the angels.

The flicks of light were coming from something powerful.

Three of those flicks of blue light entered my body. Each spark came from a young man. An image of their face flashed in my head as the spark entered my body.

While these spirits were inside me, I was in complete darkness. The most sickening feelings of trauma gripped me as I endured death.

I felt the same trauma, terror, and fear that they felt. It could not hurt me anymore than facing my own death.

I tried to leave as fast as I could. This was too much hurt to bear. I probably should have pulled off the road. I was so shaken. There's no way I was going to stop! I wanted to get as far away as I could.

From looking at their faces, I thought the spirits might be soldiers from the Civil War. All three were young men. One of them was wearing a blue cap. They were not anyone that I recognized.

Every time I pass that place, hairs rise up on the back of my neck. It's not because it is happening again. It's just that I remember those intense feelings.

I thought, *Am I having an anxiety attack?* I know that's what the doctor would call it.

That experience made me sick. My heart beat fast. Bronchitis caused my chest to tighten. I was weak and light headed. After eight days in the hospital, I still could not get out of bed.

After that trauma, I developed other problems. I had trouble swallowing. The muscles in my throat contracted. Breathing problems caused anxiety attacks. When I couldn't get my breath, I sank into a dark tunnel. I thought, *"I'm going to die"*.

I knew I had to calm myself down! That's not easy to do when you can't breathe. There is a trick to overcoming this. You cannot let yourself reach this final stage. At this point, you have reached death's door.

All of these symptoms have lasted for years. I don't get to the final stage very often, but the potential is always there. I never leave the house without anxiety medicine.

CHAPTER 12

Esther's Hospital Room 2001: Angel Escorts

*M*y mother-in-law, Esther Compton, was in the Iuka Hospital. The doctors had pulled her feeding tube. She had not eaten any food in three days. She couldn't last very much longer.

I had taken a leave from school to stay with Mrs. Compton. My husband had been her only child. I was the only family member that could care for her.

It was about ten o'clock at night. I walked to the door and looked down the hallway.

A few doors down, I saw Charles Brown. He was one of my husband's best friends. They had worked together for years. He was staying with his mother, who was a patient. I waved at him and came back into the room. I didn't leave Mrs. Compton unless someone was with her. So I didn't go talk to him. He did not cross my mind again.

After being up and down with Mrs. Compton for two days

and nights, I was exhausted! I checked on her to see how she was doing. Her breathing was easy. She seemed to be resting. Thinking I needed to sleep while I could, I lay on a cot beside her bed. She had been agitated for days. At this stage, someone had to be near her at all times.

I instantly dropped off into a deep sleep. I don't know exactly how long I slept, maybe an hour.

I was startled from my sleep by an energy that pulsated in my body. All my senses were elevated. Because these feelings were so sensual, I thought I must be dreaming.

Feeling someone in the room, I opened my eyes. I was in the presence of angels. My spirit must have seen them, because my body was lying on the cot with my eyes closed.

The light was very dim. Two men were dressed in pants, shirts, and shoes. One had on a wide-brimmed felt hat. Similar to a mist, they were a pale smoky color that was almost transparent. Their clothes were also a pale mist.

I knew one of the men was Mr. Will Seaton, Esther's father. I never met him, but I'd seen pictures of him. The other man was dressed similar to him, but I didn't recognize him. He was someone Esther knew.

They paid no attention to me. There was no communication between us.

They were here for Mrs. Compton. She was lying on the bed with her eyes closed. The two men stood at the foot of the bed. They didn't move their arms, but I could feel Mr. Seaton reaching out to her. I could see her spirit rising out of her body to meet him. She was smiling. I know she knew him.

Suddenly she fell back into her body, and the angels disappeared.

Did they realize that I was watching them? Mrs. Compton didn't die that night, but she never opened her eyes again.

I went home the next morning. My daughter, Cortney, was with her grandmother when she passed away, an hour later.

CHAPTER 13

The School Bus Incident:
The Shield

$\mathcal{O}$n the 1990s I taught kindergarten at Burnsville school. I also drove a school bus on the morning route. The school often asked me to be a substitute driver in the afternoon.

Mrs. Pat, our principal, asked me to drive Mr. Bray's bus. He was sick that day. I was a little apprehensive about this route, because I had never driven it.

Being extra cautious, I left the school and made several stops. I turned off the main highway to a gravel road. I did not have as much traffic at the bus stops on this road.

Michael Carter was a sixth-grade student that I had taught in kindergarten. He stood up to get off the bus. I knew his family well. I was very familiar with where they lived. I had been to their house several times. He said, "The next driveway is my stop." The students were always helpful with new drivers. The next driveway was just over a hill.

I drove right past that driveway, even though he had just told me where to stop. I knew his driveway as well as I knew my own. There was no reason for me to do that. The bus went at least two hundred feet past the driveway before I stopped.

I opened the bus door for Michael to get off. At that moment, an eighteen-wheel truck with a flatbed, topped the hill. It skidded to the other side of the road. By the time it stopped, it was off the road.

The driver ran to the bus and asked if anyone was hurt. I said, "We are fine. No one was injured." The truck didn't hit the bus. It didn't involve the bus in any way. That would not have been the story if I had stopped at that driveway. He could not have avoided us. The truck would have plowed into the back of the bus.

That should have been the end of the incident, just a near-missed accident. That wasn't all that I saw and heard that day. The truck made some noise as it skidded to a stop. That was nothing compared to what was behind it.

Powerful, moaning sounds were coming from a force that moved like a tornado. It contained dark, violent winds that were swirling in all directions. There were features on a face, but they were not very distinct. Its shape was similar to a dark cloud.

I was seeing this vision through someone else's eyes. I could see me sitting in the driver's seat. All the children were watching the driver. My viewpoint was from above the bus.

The truck was coming. That dark force was pushing it along at a fast speed. I stood at the back of the bus with my hands raised to stop the truck. The truck went to the side. The dark force went over the bus and left the area.

I came through the roof and down the aisle. Inside the bus, I saw myself.

My body was not an empty shell. It was not just sitting there

BETTY COMPTON

without a spirit. I was doing all the things I usually did when I drove the bus.

Yet, I was watching myself as if I were another person. I don't have a concept of what I looked like, while I was watching myself.

Quickly, I drifted down the aisle and melted into my body. It never left the driver's seat. I did not feel the sensation of leaving my body or re-entering it. It happened in a flash.

At that moment, I saw the most wonderful sight. An angel was standing in the aisle next to me. She was a spirit, not someone I could touch. She didn't look solid. A beautiful glow came from her transparent body and from the white, flowing clothing she was wearing. Her features were like a human. I noticed long blond hair, white skin, fingernails, eyebrows, and eyelashes. I saw a soft, slender, feminine body.

At the same time, she had a strong, powerful, almost on-fire look about her. I knew she was a defender or a warrior. She could vanquish an evil spirit with the touch of her finger. She was much larger than a human, about eight feet tall. There were glorious wings, but they weren't spread out. She didn't seem to need them to fly. She moved at the speed of light. There was no communication with me. But I knew things about her just by being there!

She had touched my body and caused me to move the bus out of the way! After that I was part of her. I was in her body, when she was above the bus, and when she stood behind the bus!

While I was in her body, I felt and saw things that are impossible for a human to comprehend. That dark force was not meant for human sight. I was conscious of an area all around the bus. My vision was not just in front of my eyes. It was all-knowing and all-seeing.

The smallest details were visible to me. I could feel the rubber that came off the truck tires, when they skidded to a stop. I knew all of the children's thoughts and feelings. I also felt every bump or contact the children had on the bus. The information that I knew about the dark spirit and the angel, I learned while I was in her body.

In a split second, she was gone. I was back to being my very limited self.

Touching that angel did not hurt my physical body at all. It actually seemed to boost my health. I did not have any aches or pains for months.

I was as cool as a cucumber when I finished that bus route. What I experienced was very traumatic. Touching that angel was healing. Instead of accelerating it, this episode took away all of my anxiety.

As I was returning to school with an empty bus, I passed a wreck on Highway 365. Later I heard a man had a heart attack. He died when his car ran off the road and caught on fire. As I listened to a news report of the wreck, the thought of that dark force crossed my mind.

The school bus

CHAPTER 14

My Sister-in-Law's Death:
A Vision

My brother, David, and his wife, Terry, lived three hours away from my house. They had recently moved to Hamilton, Alabama. I seldom saw them. I had been to their house a couple of times since they moved. They were both working long hours and they could not drive home often.

One morning in March, I was upstairs doing my normal daily housekeeping; laundry, floors, and beds.

All of a sudden, I felt a strange sensation. All of my senses became very keen. I felt a slight shock. My body tingled with small pulsating vibes. What a strange sensation! It was a little painful and pleasant at the same time.

I felt like energy went through me. I thought it must be electricity. "Did I touch a live wire?"

At that exact moment, a picture of Terry's face flashed in my head. Her eyes were wide open, and she had a strange look on her face. I could not see any of her surroundings. I felt more than I saw.

A few minutes later, I got a telephone call. My sister-in-law was dead! "Had I witnessed her death?"

My brother had been cleaning a gun. He hit the wooden stock of the gun with the palm of his hand. He intended to tighten it. The gun went off and shot Terry in the chest.

I saw the expression on her face, when she was shot. I probably felt what she felt. I had a sense of shock, and then a calm peace came over me.

David and Terry had rented my mother-in-law's house for about a year. At the time I was teaching kindergarten, driving a school bus, and managing rent property. I also had two school aged daughters and a sick grandmother to care for. I had to have some help!

Terry became Grandma Compton's nurse. She came to my house every day. She cooked, cleaned, and took wonderful care of her.

David had a job, but he helped me with repairs and maintenance. To help pay Grandma Compton's nursing fees, I let them live in her house rent free. Grandma loved David and Terry. They made her last days enjoyable.

They were also a big help to me. I couldn't keep my job and give her the care she needed. Grandma didn't want to go to the nursing home. Without David and Terry, I would have had no other choice but to put her there.

Grandma Compton had lived by herself for the past ten years. She always kept a loaded gun in her laundry room, near the back door. That loaded gun had been there for at least thirty years.

Even when her husband was alive, he worked out of town

most of the time. For years, he worked in Hammond, Indiana on the steel mills. He only came home on holidays. She and her son practically lived alone for ten years. She was prepared to take care of herself.

David and Terry cleaned out Grandma Compton's belongings. They brought most of them to my house. We knew she would never move back home.

They remodeled the house. I gave David the gun, and a lot more of her things, for the work he was doing. They lived in the house until Grandma passed away in 2001. After that, they bought a place of their own and moved to Alabama.

CHAPTER 15

The Basketball Game:
Spiritual Encounter

*M*y husband died on January 9,1994. Even though his death was very traumatic, my spirit did not leave my body, and I didn't encounter an angel at the time of his death. I did have a spiritual experience about six weeks later.

Harvey loved to watch our youngest daughter play basketball. She played on the seventh- and eighth-grade teams. Harvey never missed any of her games.

He played basketball when he was in school. He never had time to coach, but he loved to advise Casey.

One day he saw that she was having trouble with a teammate. Both players wanted to do all the shooting. Casey complained to her daddy that the other girl would not pass her the ball.

He told her, "Every time you get the ball, pass it to that girl."

Doing that for a week ended the quarrel over the ball. The other girl started passing to Casey. They started working as a team. They worked better together than any other team members.

Casey had a particular place that she made three-point shots. If she got a shot from that spot, she usually made the basket. Her coach called plays to get her there in almost every game. Sometimes Harvey held up three fingers when she was going for a three pointer. He watched her games up to the week he died.

Although Harvey had been sick, his death was unexpected. On January 3, 1994 he entered the hospital with stomach problems. We knew he was sick, but he was walking, talking, and eating fine.

On Saturday night, I left him with his mother and came home. I was going to bring the girls to the hospital the next morning.

I called and talked to him at eight o'clock on Sunday morning. I told him we were getting ready to come to the hospital. He said, "No, take the girls to church. Come after lunch. Momma will stay with me."

The girls talked to their daddy. He never hung up before he told us he loved us. That was the last "I love you" we heard from Harvey.

We stopped at a restaurant to eat breakfast before church. While we were there, I got a call.

Harvey died one hour after we talked to him.

The girls and I went back to school a week later. We were getting back in our normal routine. We missed him, but staying busy helps with your grief.

One day I was in the kindergarten classroom when I felt tingly all over. All my senses were heightened. I could hear conversations down the hall. I saw the whole school at one time. The principal was in his office. My class was checking out books. Awareness of the smallest details filled my head. I noticed fire ants in the cracks around the sidewalk. I was even aware of the electricity running through the wires.

I felt a quickening energy pass through my body with an intensity so great, it was almost painful. Emotions were also painful because of their intensity.

It was after two o'clock. Casey had ball practice in the gym at that time.

My spirit was in the gym, looking down at Harvey sitting on the top bleacher. That was his normal place to sit when he watched Casey play ball. The whole length of the gym was in my view. There was Casey, playing below me. Harvey was watching her. Three fingers went up. He said, "Make one for me".

In a flash I was back in my body, which had never left the kindergarten classroom. I was writing spelling words on the board.

After I came back, I began to tremble and cry hysterically. Tears were rolling down my cheeks uncontrollably. The marker fell, and I couldn't write another word. The super sense had passed. I was left shaken.

My class was at the library with my assistant. They could not see me in such a shape. I had to get a substitute driver to take my bus route. The school nurse drove me home. She said all the stress of losing a love one had probably been building in me. It just hit me all at once. I didn't tell her I was feeling emotions at ten times their normal intensity.

My sister drove me to my doctor. He prescribed anxiety medicine. It did calm me down and allowed me to sleep. That episode happened on Wednesday. I was not able to return to work until the following Monday.

Casey was helping me set the table for dinner that night. She said, "I thought I saw Daddy watching me at practice today. I glanced up and he was there. The next time I looked he was gone."

I told her, "I am sure he would love to be there."

CHAPTER 16

Out-of-Body Experience

I had been sick for a week with bronchitis. A rattling cough and tightness in my chest led to anxiety and a lack of sleep—the usual symptoms I had with bronchitis. The symptoms were really extreme this time. I had suffered with this lung condition for over thirty years. Every time I got a cold, it usually turned into bronchitis.

That morning, I got up and made my coffee. My dog, Lucy, scratched at the door. She was ready for a walk. Although I was sluggish, I wasn't feeling that bad. As I walked Lucy, I sipped my coffee. I did absolutely nothing different from my ordinary routine.

Bam! I fell to the ground.

I felt myself descending into a silent, dark tunnel. Almost immediately, I left the tunnel and popped out of my body. A thin, airy version of me had all the features that my body possessed. It also had a few new features. I could fly.

As I moved away, this strange image of me started to disintegrate. I was still me, but I was becoming part of the world around me. At this point, I was probably one hundred feet above my body.

There I was, dressed in pajamas lying on the ground. Lucy dragged her leash as she ran down the hill. At a slow, steady pace, I floated upward, past the treetops and into the sky. I could see my front yard and my backyard at the same time. As I moved higher, the body lying on the ground became doll-sized.

My soul, my memories, my intellect, and my feelings were all in that being above my body. All of me was there. The body lying on the ground was an empty package. It was void of life. It contained nothing that had to do with me. It didn't contain any more of me than a log of wood.

Out-of-Body Experience

In a very short time, I came back to earth. Pausing merely inches from my face, I melted back into my body. After opening my eyes, I got up and walked to the house. I called, "Mom, come and take me to the hospital. I must be having a heart attack."

After a lot of tests, the doctors told me it wasn't a heart attack or a stroke.

Every time I've had an out-of-body experience, it has weakened me. Although this spell only lasted a few seconds, it caused the most physical damage.

I've suffered with muscle weakness, slurred speech, and loss of memory. I've also experienced high anxiety and rapid heart palpitations. All these maladies started after this experience. They didn't stop. They have continued for three years in varying degrees.

Sometimes I am almost normal. At other times I can't get out of bed. I had to retire within a month of this experience. I was not able to teach school or drive a bus.

The greatest amount of damage to my body seems to come from out-of-body-experiences. Could this be caused by lack of oxygen? Does my body start to deteriorate when my spirit leaves it? Is damage done from the shock of the spirit separating from the body? All I have is questions. I have no answers.

The Beach House

I've had a history of fainting since I was a girl. I don't usually leave my body when I faint.

On one of my trips to the emergency room, my diagnosis was a vagal experience. The artery to my heart collapsed for a few seconds. It is not serious as a heart attack. That's what was cutting off the flow of blood from my heart to my brain. That may not be what happens each time I faint. On that day, a vagal experience was the culprit. Vagal experience is just a medical term for fainting.

This episode was triggered by pain and a little anxiety. My daughter's family and I were spending a week on the beach in Destin, Florida.

With panic in her voice, my daughter called from the upstairs condo, "Where's Gavin?" I immediately started searching outside for the toddler. Pool, beach, road ... No Gavin!

As I rushed around, I caught my fingers in the garage door. It just pinched them a little. That scare and pain was enough to send me into the dark tunnel. I passed out!

As I floated into that silent darkness, I thought, *I'm dying! I'm never going to see my grand babies again.* That's a scare that causes a high level of anxiety. You can't breathe. Your chest hurts. You think you are having a heart attack.

This crisis didn't last but a minute or two. Little Gavin was in the next room. Normally, this incident would not phase me at all. It might cause my heart to beat a little fast—nothing more than a little exercise would cause.

It should not take me to death's door. I never know when the conditions are right for this to happen. I don't even have a clue to what these conditions are.

There are many physical triggers that cause my spirit to separate from my body. Most have to do with pain, lack of oxygen, drugs, high anxiety, and fear. I also think conditions have to be right for these things to trigger the separation. I have experienced all of these triggers when they didn't cause my body to separate from my spirit. Most of the time they don't affect me in any abnormal way.

I have had several high-anxiety situations in which I kept my cool. In fact, it is not my nature to panic. During an accident or a crisis, I am usually the level-headed one.

Leaving my body starts out like fainting, and then it becomes so much more. At this point, the blackout goes from being caused by something physical (a lack of oxygen) to something spiritual. My spirit separates from my body. It rises above it. Gravity doesn't hold it to the earth. All of my thinking and talking abilities are in that spirit. I am in that spirit. My body is an empty shell that is left behind. I am weightless and free.

The further I go from my body, the better I feel. Everything is beautiful, peaceful, and painless. The longer I stay away, the less I want to return.

There is a progression in my experiences. First is fainting. I start traveling into a dark hole. Second, my spirit leaves my body. I travel through the dark hole and come out above my body. Third is the near-death experience. I travel into the dark hole. I come out and rise above my body. I travel into a bright light, where everything is intensified and beautiful.

I have never reached step four. I think it is death. I have come as close to death as anyone can, and live.

For thirty years, my doctors wanted to prescribe anti-depressants and anxiety medicine! I know they saw physical damage from stress and anxiety.

At first, I would not take any anxiety medicine because of the job I did. Bus drivers are tested often for drugs. But that wasn't the only reason. I needed to be in control of myself. I couldn't let anything lessen that control.

I was also scared of the way drugs affected me. Something as simple as the sight of blood made me faint. I remember fainting when I pulled a tooth and looked at the little bit of blood on it.

Being put to sleep really scared me. I tend to leave my body under anesthesia. Any mind-altering drug is not an option for me.

For thirty years, I had to find other ways to handle stress and anxiety. I had to avoid the triggers that caused my spirit to leave my body.

Friends helped. I have a couple of close friends who are always there when I need them. My mom and sisters are always ready for a girls' day out. I've always stayed active. My grandchildren never fail to keep me interested in life. I've never had a lonely day. I've never had a day with nothing to do.

There is one thing that gave me the most strength. I learned to ask for God's help: then I learned to accept his help.

My job was also my salvation. It is impossible to be anxious and depressed when you teach kindergarten. You're engaged with students every second of the school day. They not only learn the knowledge you impart—your mood, tone, and manner determine how they learn. A positive attitude not only helps the students, but it also helps you cope with your own problems.

Driving a bus is a therapy session in itself. If you think all you have to do is sit there and drive, you are fantasizing. I found the best discipline was to greet each child by his or her name. Connecting with your students and giving of yourself helps to overcome stress.

The Pig Barn

The first time I remember leaving my body was in the summer of my tenth year. I was spending the weekend with one of Mom's cousins. Daddy was on a drunk. We often left home when that happened. Even though they had been divorced for two years, Daddy would not leave us alone.

We stayed with Mom's cousin, Dean. Daddy wouldn't come to his house. Dean had worked in law enforcement and he would not tolerate a drunk.

My cousins lived in a small community called Valley. Many of Mom's family were buried there. Mom never failed to go to church on Decoration Day. Once a year, they had a gospel singing, preaching, and dinner on the ground. We always decorated the graves. This year, we decided to spend the weekend.

This was the closest thing to a vacation that we did. I couldn't have enjoyed it any more if it had been a five-star resort.

Staying at my cousins' house was like being at a summer camp. They swam. They rode horses. We even had a campfire in their backyard. Their mom cooked good food. Most of it was food they raised. Her chicken and biscuits were wonderful. Of course, I didn't watch her go to the chicken pen and dress young fryers to cook.

I thought my cousins were so smart. If they wanted something, they just made it themselves. They taught me to walk on tom walkers that they made from branches of small trees. I guess I admired their independence.

There was so much to do there. I was amazed at all the fun they had. They worked hard, but they knew how to earn their own money.

Mom told me to stay close to the house. Daddy could be close by. I had two cousins who were about my age. I went to the barn with them while they did their chores. I loved their farm. I helped feed chickens, horses, and pigs.

We saddled up the horses. I had to ride with them. I had never been on a horse before. People did a lot of trail riding in their area. They lived near a state park that was famous for its trails. Although they were just eleven and thirteen years old, they had been on horses all their lives. The trail we followed was close to their home. The horses circled rocks that were bigger than houses. It was so beautiful. I felt so happy and carefree. I totally forgot about Daddy for a little while.

After the ride, my cousin Sandy and I climbed into the barn loft. The barn floor was full of young pigs. She wanted to show me the pigs from the loft. Hay was stored on each side. There was no floor over the main hallway. Six-by-twelve beams spanned the opened ceiling.

Sandy did not have to walk those beams to get to the other side. Each side had a ladder. I think she wanted to sit on the open beams and watch the pigs below. It was not my cousin's first time to be in that barn loft. Unlike me, she walked those beams like a mountain goat. When I tried to follow her, I fell twelve feet.

I don't know exactly why I fell. I may have lost my balance. I may have fainted because of a fear of heights.

The very second I fell, I looked down. I saw Sandy standing on the beam. She was below me. Her hand went to her mouth in shock, and she screamed. I saw my body lying on the ground, with the pigs around me. That body was lifeless. It was still and silent. I was high enough to see the whole length of the barn. After a few seconds, I was back in my body.

I fell on my right arm. The bone was broken and dislocated. I must have passed out. When I woke up, I was in a car. Dean was driving me to the doctor.

I passed out again when they pulled that bone back in place.

That was the first time my spirit left my body. It was thirty years before that happened again. All the other out-of-body experiences happened after I was fifty years old.

CHAPTER 17

The Beauty Queen: Angel Encounter

*M*y oldest daughter, Cortney got married in 2003. Her husband, Alvin joined the air force just before they married. After training he was stationed at Tinker Air Force Base in Oklahoma City. He expected to be there for four years. Cortney packed all their things and joined him in Oklahoma.

I was busy teaching school. I drove the ten-hour trip from my house in Tishomingo County, Mississippi, to Oklahoma City every time I had a holiday.

I worried about Cortney. She started having pain in her bladder. At the time, she thought she was having kidney infections. That was something she had suffered with since high school.

A doctor had diagnosed her with interstitial cystitis a couple of years earlier. She started seeing a doctor near her new home. His treatments helped her. For years she had been taking antibiotics, which only inflamed her bladder. They never got rid of the problem. She was thrilled. "Finally, I've found someone who is helping me."

Cortney's whole personality was changing. She had finished college with a degree in elementary education. She only worked a few weeks as a substitute teacher. Normally she loved working with kids. She lost interest in getting a teaching job. At first she was too sick, and then she got pregnant. Her interstitial cystitis got better while she was pregnant but came back stronger than ever after the baby was born.

I always suspected that her diet and medicine caused her bladder problems. I never worried about alcohol because it would set her on fire. She wouldn't drink cokes or any kind of citrus. She wasn't anorexic, but she eliminated a lot of whole food groups from her diet. She starved herself of nutrients that her body needed. And she had been taking prescribed antibiotics for years. I think both contributed to her bladder problem.

Cortney's obsession with looking good started when she was fourteen. She was always looking for ways to eliminate fat from her diet. I told her she didn't need to lose weight. Most of the time, she was so interested in everyone around her, she didn't dwell on herself. But she was the typical pageant girl. She would do what it takes to look good.

Cortney won a lot of beauty pageants from high school through college. She was also in the Miss Mississippi Pageant and preliminaries to the Miss America program.

Cortney had so much love and compassion for people. She did a platform on grief counseling for children. For two years, she worked in Disney's Make-a-Wish Program. It was a foundation for terminally ill children. Business and charity events could always count on her to perform and support their cause.

Cortney's Community Chats featured someone from the community each week in the local newspaper. That article was enjoyed by the young and the old. Many knew her from the articles she wrote. There was not anyone in our county who didn't love Cortney.

She was a social butterfly who was withdrawing into a self-made cocoon. The first apartment they lived in was decorated so well, the landlords used it to show prospective tenants. Everything was beautiful. She took care of every detail. That perfection changed. The second one was a cluttered mess. Cortney was getting more depressed.

After their second child was born, anti-depressants were prescribed for post-partum depression. Along with the medicine came the interstitial cystitis. She was admitted to the hospital to stretch the tube that goes from the kidney to the bladder. The doctors had also found some cancerous cells that they wanted to check out.

The hospital stay was supposed to be for one day—just an outpatient-type thing. When they went into her bladder, it looked like raw meat with torn lesions. Fentanyl and a morphine drip were administered for pain. When they took that out, she was given a strong time-release pain patch and sent home. Cortney, who could not even take aspirin, had anti-depressants and strong pain killers in her.

The next morning, Alvin could not wake her up. He called 911. When they got her to the hospital she was barely breathing and in a deep coma.

After ten days we were losing hope! The doctors told us fluid was collecting around her heart, her kidneys were failing, her left side was paralyzed, and blood was settling in her feet. Some of my family had been at the hospital with us since Cortney was admitted.

On the tenth day, Alvin's brother and his first cousin came. Her mother had laid in the hospital with a brain injury from a car wreck. She didn't recover from it. I guess that's why she went with Alvin to talk to the doctor. She had been in this situation before.

In a few minutes, Alvin and his cousin came back to the waiting room, where I was waiting. He said, "We're going to take her off the breathing machine. The doctor says there's no hope for her."

That almost killed me! I started crying and fell to my knees. I felt like I had the breath knocked out of me. No! No! No! I couldn't listen to them. I couldn't lose my baby!

My spirit left my body. From the ceiling, I looked down at everyone in the waiting room. The thought of losing Cortney was the greatest hurt I had ever felt. They kept talking like I was still there. Alvin tried to put his arms around me. He tried to comfort me. I could not speak. All I could do was cry.

While I was out of my body, a young lady walked down the hall and looked up at the ceiling where I was. She wore high heels shoes and was dressed in a white suit with a tight skirt. Her long hair was straight and glowed with a shimmer, as it hung past her shoulders. Her nails were manicured, and she was perfectly groomed. She looked like Cortney in a pageant interview. She also had another look. A white, misty light radiated from her. A peaceful, contented look was on her face.

I first thought, *oh no, Cortney's dead, and this is her spirit.* She didn't speak; she simply looked at me. I immediately felt a calm peace. I did not hurt anymore—not even a little bit. I understood her message clearly. I knew who she was. She was an angel that was sent to give me a message.

I knew all about what was happening in Cortney's body. I

could see the blood going through her arteries. While I watched, it started moving faster. It wasn't dark. It became a brilliant, glowing, vibrant liquid. It was every color that you could imagine. I could smell a sweet scent going through her body. I knew it was life.

Cortney was healing. Prayers for her were being answered. Even without speaking a word, the beauty queen gave me a great awareness and peace. I knew the feelings and thoughts of everyone in the waiting room. Alvin was thinking, *this is hard to say, but I've got to man up and do it.*

The doctor was thinking. *"Who is this woman with Cortney's husband?" I should have talked to her mother and husband. She's not family. He should not just come out and say. Cortney's dying. I don't know if her mother can stand the shock.*

I could feel the pity from a passing nurse. She watched me sobbing, and a thought of her own daughter flashed in her head. "I need to get her a Kleenex." She wished she could do something to help. I looked down at myself, crying hysterically.

The beauty queen disappeared when I went back into my body. The experience must not have lasted more than a few seconds. Everyone was still talking about what the doctor said. I was back to normal. The beauty queen was gone. Her message and the most wonderful peace stayed with me.

The Beauty Queen

I waited very calmly as they took the breathing machine off. She didn't die. Cortney was breathing on her own. Later that day, we saw a little eye twitch and some finger movement when she was pricked.

I actually lay down and slept that night. I remembered singing a hymn in church about "The peace that passes all understanding." I knew I must be feeling it that night. I went into an empty room and prayed, which was something I could not do before.

I pondered, *Did the thought of Cortney's death cause me to go into shock? Did the shock cut off the oxygen to my brain? While I may have questioned why my spirit departed my body. I have no doubts about the angel or the miracle she brought.*

I cannot deny the peace I felt. I knew Cortney was in God's hands. I could accept his will, whatever the outcome was.

The next morning, Alvin's daddy went into the ICU for the first five-minute visitation of the day. It was about four o'clock in the morning. Everyone else was asleep. Cortney opened her eyes and spoke to him. She was awake long enough to say, "Where's my husband?".

She came out of the coma after eleven days. It was a miracle!

Cortney was in and out of hospitals for the next two years. She had to have a lot of physical therapy and rehabilitation. She had to learn to walk again. Her left side was paralyzed. Recovery was long and hard. But she lived through it, with a lot of help.

The beauty queen told me my prayers were answered. I'm ashamed to say it, but they were not my prayers. Sometimes when you're hurting, it's hard to pray.

I did not have the faith to put it in God's hands. I closed myself off from any help. No one could help me. I was scared and full of anger. "How could this happen to my precious daughter?"

No one could help me, and I couldn't help myself! I didn't put it in words, but I was angry with God.

When someone would call and ask, "What can we do?" we would say "Pray for her."

Prayers came from Mississippi and Oklahoma. She also had friends from college, Disney, and pageants praying. Members from the air force visited and prayed daily.

Someone from the Norman, Oklahoma, church stayed with us every day. They never left without praying for our family.

Cortney's recovery was because of answered prayers! I didn't have to hear it from an angel to believe that.

CHAPTER 18

The Celestial Sense

*W*hen I was a child, I did not acknowledge the fact that unusual things were happening to me. As I grew older, I began to question my strange experiences. I thought about angels. I also wondered if I had been drugged. My greatest fear was that I was slipping into insanity.

As more strange things occurred, I really wanted to find out what was happening to me. Since I didn't have a clue at this time, I began reading books about psychics, angel sightings, and out-of-body experiences. Almost every account had something that was similar to my spiritual episodes. No experience was exactly like mine.

Disagreement always came when the authors started giving their opinions about what happened to them. Many gave explanations as truth, that were actually just opinions.

After the years of living with Harvey and experiencing his manic behavior, I decided stress was the culprit. I was beginning to think these experiences were all stress related. I even wondered if my personality was one that was attracted to this kind of situation. When I had the near-death experience, I became aware of angels. I knew it wasn't all stress.

I am and have always been a skeptic with anything psychic! There's got to be a logical answer! I've searched diligently for that answer. I've read and reread every verse in the Bible that mentions angels.

I've also studied research on esthetic seizures and changes in the brain during out-of-body experiences! For twenty years I've been interested in any information that concerned a spiritual departure from the body.

After Cortney came out of the coma, the doctors said she had suffered an anoxic brain injury. She had some brain damage caused by lack of oxygen. Of course, I wondered if that could have been what happened to me. I may have an anoxic brain injury. I definitely experienced a lack of oxygen.

There is a lot of research that believes these types of experiences are caused by a physical reason. Past experiences and overstimulated senses are some of the explanations. I believe physical reasons start the episodes. But at some point, it is no longer physical. It becomes spiritual!

In every near- death experience each person came to the same conclusion! Most saw the light, and they realized it came from God.

As a spirit, I possessed many abilities that most humans do not have. I cannot describe all of them. Here are a few that I can give a name to:

- Empathy—the ability to feel others' emotions
- Telepathy—a way of communicating thoughts from one person's mind to another without using words

- Clairvoyance—remote viewing—perception outside human senses
- Psychometry—obtaining information about a person by touching them
- Astral Projection—mind is separated from your body
- Retro-cognition—perception of past events

A few times, I had some of these abilities when I was not in a spiritual form. These psychic abilities are not natural to me. I was not born with them. They are a result of either the departures from my body or from the angel encounters. They are all part of the celestial sense—a sense that all the angels possess.

I am a Christian. These brief experiences have not taken away any of my belief in God. In fact, they have only made it clearer. I don't think I have any new message from God. I do think God uses us as an instrument to help others. People, spirits, and angels all play a part in carrying out God's will. We just don't realize all the help we have.

It seems strange that I have remembered even small details that have taken place over a fifty-year span. It's as if they were permanently imprinted into my brain! I can't remember anything about events that are really important to me—for example, my daughter's wedding, or the birth of my grandchildren. Normally I remember the big things, but I forget the details.

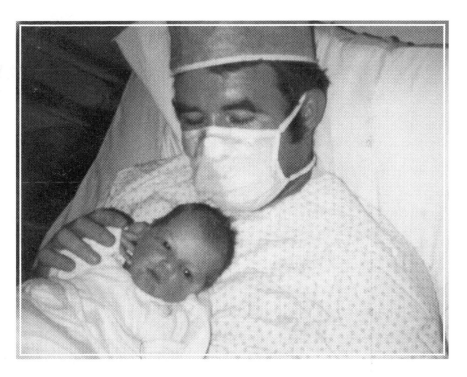

Harvey with our second daughter, Casey

The birth of my second daughter, Casey, was one of the most beautiful memories I have. I watched as she came into this world. I heard her first cry. As I held her in my arms, I felt warm feelings of love—feelings I should never forget. Even though these feelings were intense, they are fading.

I've lost the details, even though they were so precious to me. I can't relive it. The reason is because I experienced this moment with my human senses. The events in my book were experienced with a celestial sense. I remember them as if they happened yesterday.

We can't condemn others. We only see what affects us. God sees the whole picture. We see bad things that happen and wonder why. Disease, cruelty, anger, wars, hunger, and death are all things of this world. We will not experience these awful things when we are with God. All the hurts of this world disappeared when I came close to God.

Did I see God? I don't think I looked at his face and body. I don't think you can do that and live. I do think I felt God and saw him through the angels and the light. When I came close to death, I came closer to God. That's what enlightened my spirit. When I moved away from God and came back to earth, I lost that enlightenment.

Did I go to heaven when I had my near-death experience? No, I didn't enter heaven. I was close to it. Heaven is a place where God is. Even though I saw God all around me, my human spirit could not enter the home of God and the angels. It's impossible to do that and come back to earth as a human. Even when a spirit leaves the human body, it's still just a human spirit.

Although I was in a spiritual form, I never changed from a human spirit to a heavenly spirit. Human spirits do not leave this world and go directly to heaven.

There are a few examples in the Bible that could be examples of a human spirit instantly changing to a heavenly spirit. Elijah never saw death (2 Kings 2:11).

In the last days some will be changed in the twinkling of an eye (1 Corinthians 15:52).

Jesus said to the thief on the cross, "Today you will be with me in paradise" (Luke 23:43).

Most of us will not change to heavenly spirits instantly. Most will experience death.

The episodes in which my spirit left my body, did give me a few insights to the process of death. That knowledge is but a teardrop compared to an ocean, in the infinity of God's spiritual world. So this is speculation on my part.

I think death begins when your spirit leaves your body. You travel through a spiritual realm that contains God's light. The gates of heaven represent a barrier between the human spirit and the heavenly spirit. After God changes you into a heavenly spirit, only then can you enter heaven.

God's light is in us. We are able to see that light, so we are able to see God. Even though I could see more of him as a spirit, that didn't scratch the surface when it comes to having knowledge of God. It did not give me answers to questions we all have. I don't think it is meant for humans to keep the celestial knowledge they acquire as spirits. We have to believe by faith!

I didn't see God as one body. He was the light. As a spirit, I saw a dim light in all humans. In some it was brighter than others. On earth, I didn't sense any light in the world around us. The light was in our spirit. When I left my body, there was no light in that empty shell. As my spirit moved away from earth, God grew stronger, and the light became brighter.

God was in everything. He was in the soil, sky, water, plants, and animals.

This beautiful place looked like earth, but it also looked heavenly. There was land, water, and plants. The place looked heavenly because of the light, beauty, and serenity. The spirits were the image of their earthly bodies. I thought it might be a place you waited until you could enter heaven.

Prayer is a way we can communicate with God. He already knows every thought and feeling we have. Prayer helps us to know our innermost feelings. We are like a camera out of focus. Communicating with God puts things into focus.

After I retired, I started working on my family ancestry. I studied the history of the Scotch Irish people who settled in America in the 1700s. These people lost their land, property, families, and religious freedom. All their struggles and suffering caused them to develop the ideals that this country was founded on—a government for the people, by the people, no government-run churches, the right to bear arms. As you look back over the years, you can see the whole picture. The bad things that happened to them were part of God's plan for America.

What makes me able to see these spirits? Coming into contact with angels sharpened my senses and ability to see them.

Are my angel encounters and out-of-body-experiences connected? Could they be two separate ways to reach a spiritual form? Did one cause the other to happen?

Angels have entered my body for a few brief instances. I saw the angel on the school bus when she pressed my foot on the gas. I couldn't see her before she touched me. I could not see angels until after I touched Harvey in the near-death experience.

I was able to see the dark spirit in the psychiatric hospital, only because the Indian angel was nearby. The dark being behind the bus was viewed because the warrior angel was near me.

That Indian angel made me realize that we are all God's children. He loves all of humankind. I'm not saying that there's no need for God's plan of salvation. There was a need for Jesus to come to earth and provide us with a means to eternal life. But that's not to say all of humankind are not his children. God is in all of his children. He has been in contact with them throughout history.

How do we become a spirit? Or how do these spirits enter our bodies? For me, every time I left my body, it was because of a lack of oxygen to my brain, extreme fear and anxiety, or injury and pain. For my daddy, the door opener was alcohol. Drugs do it for many. Pain, fear, stress, and injuries are often the physical cause. Prayer and meditation work for some people. For Harvey, I think it was a chemical imbalance in his brain. Reactions to sleeping medicine caused the attack.

Prescription drugs really scare me. I've always been afraid to take any medicine, especially mind altering drugs. I never know how something as simple as an aspirin or a glass of wine is going to affect me.

In some people, at certain times, any drug can open a spiritual door that will let a demon come through. That thought alone is enough to get you classified as mentally ill. If your spirit has departed your body, you have to be concerned with this danger.

You never know when you are going into another spiritual realm or what is going to trigger a spiritual departure.

Because you have been a spirit, you are able to absorb both good and evil energy. Because it is so powerful, you have to stay in control.

I don't know where the dark spirits come from. I didn't see any in the place I entered when my spirit left my body. There was no darkness where the light is.

If you let evil enter your life, you let your guard down. If you let something control you (drugs, alcohol, money, hatred), you are letting your guard down. Our thoughts, actions, and emotions affect the condition of our spirit. Sin and darkness separates us from God.

Although good repels evil, that is not always the case! I have never known a purer spirit than Harvey. He was a moral person, with a huge capacity for love— for God, his family, and his brothers. If he could be possessed by a dark spirit, anyone can. When I read about good people doing horrible things, I wonder if it is a dark spirit.

On a trip to Greece, I visited Delphi, the home of the oracle of Greek myths. I learned the oracle was not one person but many young virgin girls. The well at Delphi was high in the mountains. It was a small cavern that went deep into the earth. A toxic gas was emitted through that well. When they had a client, the young girl would sit in the cavern of the well, breathe the gas, and become the oracle. She could predict the future and answer difficult questions. This gas supposedly opened the door to another spiritual realm. I wondered if it was a near-death experience that gave her these abilities.

I also wondered why they only used young virgin girls. Their lives were not valued as much as boys. The boys were educated and trained to be athletes and the girls weren't.

Or was it because they thought these young girls were clean and pure, and that they would contact good spirits and avoid the evil ones?

I don't think I became an oracle when I had my experience, but I see some similar abilities. It also made me realize these experiences have been happening for a long time. Mine was not the first time it happened.

Our human brains cannot grasp all the knowledge that I encountered in my very brief spiritual form. Not even our most advanced computers could contain it. It is impossible to describe the mental awareness I felt with mere words. I knew the tiniest details about things around me. I also had vast knowledge of God, heaven, and the world.

The same thing is true for my senses. I felt so much more than our meager five human senses could see, hear, smell, taste, and feel. I also had another sense! Even though these senses were very exaggerated, I didn't have to use them. I could communicate without speaking! I could read people's thoughts without hearing them. Their feelings and emotions became mine. I call it a celestial sense!

Of all the angels I saw, no two angels looked alike. I think they have heavenly bodies. Sometimes we see them in these bodies. When I saw the angel at the school bus, she was in her heavenly form with wings and flowing robes. When angels come to earth, they can take on the form of their former bodies. The Indian was in his earthly form.

They can also take on a form that is familiar to you. The beauty queen was in a form I recognized. In the near-death experience, I laid my head on Harvey's shoulder. That feeling of love and contentment was precious to me. Could that be why the angel revealed himself to me in such a tender manner?

I think God sometimes uses ordinary people as angels. He fills them with an angel spirit. I suspect the Kenan's were angels. They were the couple that helped us escape my daddy.

When I had the near-death experience, I envisioned an angel from my past. I say envisioned, because I did not see her with my human eyes. I saw her with a celestial sense. I call it celestial because the angels possess it.

I envisioned the angel that helped me when I was six years old. She was a young girl. I did not see any wings, but she had a soft glow about her. She came to help me. That was the only angel I revisited in my past.

The other episodes where I suspected an angel was present, were not visually seen. I never saw an angel during the car wreck, the baby's death, or the manic attack. All of these episodes happened before the near-death experience. After the near-death experience, I visually saw angels in Esther's hospital room, behind the school bus, and in the hospital when Cortney was sick.

Using this celestial sense has consequences! It causes trauma to your body. It pushes your body past its physical limits. It is so much more than your body is capable of enduring. The only reason my body endured such a force is because the light had healing properties. The light took away all my hurts and pains. This was true of the light I saw as a spirit, as well as the light from the angels.

Several dark spirits have made themselves known to me. I call them dark because I don't think they are angels. There is no light in them. I know very little about them. I only sensed their presence. Their form and thoughts are hidden from me. A dark spirit was present in four different encounters: during the manic episode, in the psychiatric hospital, on the highway, and behind the school bus.

I visually saw an image of dark spirits in only two of these experiences. I saw the spirit in the girl at the psychiatric hospital. I also saw a dark spirit behind the school bus.

I only saw the dark spirit when an angel was near. Was I seeing through an angel's eyes? Do angels see all spirits, the way we see other humans?

Dark spirits can possess humans. I saw this in the woman in the psychiatric hospital. That was the only body I saw that contained a dark spirit. Angels can also possess humans.

Where did my celestial sense come from? When I came in close contact with an angel, I received this sense. I could see spirits. I could see the past, present, and future. A super sense made me aware of everything around me. I communicated without words. Vast amounts of knowledge, feelings, and sensitivity were accessible to me. Angels get their power from the light. The light is God.

CHAPTER 19

My Later Years

So far, my sixties have been the calmest and most peaceful years of my life. My spirit has not left my body in four years. I have not seen a spirit or had any traumatic experiences in over ten years.

I am making an effort to reduce the anxiety in my life. All of my responsibilities have been reduced. I retired from all the jobs I held and sold my rent property. Now my main job is spending time with my grandchildren. It's also the thing that brings me the most pleasure.

Although I still have health problems that are related to these spiritual encounters, I am overcoming them. When I am tired, I have seizures that cause mild tremors and slurred speech. I often lose my balance.

I am not any worse than I was four years ago. These symptoms started the last time my spirit left my body. I have learned to pace myself and decrease anxiety. I don't know if the problem is any better. There's damage that I cannot improve. I have just learned to control it better.

I think I am much wiser in my older years. My many blessings are always on my mind. Thankfulness for those blessings fill my heart.

My eyes have been opened to a spiritual realm that contains God and eternity. There's nothing that can be more enlightening than that. Nothing can give you more hope for eternal life. This knowledge made me see the importance of being a Christian. There's nothing more important in this life than preparing for heaven.

Stress has not been completely erased from my life. I worry about what the future holds for my children and grandchildren. As long as I am in this world, I know I will have some worries and woes. Now I try to concentrate on the important things in life. Living a Christian life and serving my family and friends have become my top priorities.

I have learned a few life lessons from my experiences. They are just a few things that have been emphasized in my life. It's nothing you have not heard before.

(1) Every day is a gift.
By uplifting others, we uplift our own spirits. Even in the darkest times, there is something to be thankful for.

(2) Forgiveness frees you from bondage.
Hatred makes you a hostage. Sometimes the hardest person to forgive is yourself. If you are able to accept love, you will be able to give love— for God or mankind. It is true for both!

(3) Inside each of us is the potential for good and evil.
We have two flames. One flame is good, and the other flame is evil. The one that grows strong in us is the one we feed and nurture. Some of the good qualities are love, generosity,

forgiveness, patience, and virtue. Some evil qualities are hatred, lust, jealousy, greed, and vengeance. We feed these with our thoughts, actions, and emotions. To keep our spirits clean, we need to fan the good flame.

Do the angels want me to write this book? I didn't have an angel speak to me or tell me to write it. Still, I am a little suspicious about the way it came about. Was I struck down for a reason?

For years I've lived a very active lifestyle. Most of the things I read or wrote were work related. I could never sit still long enough to write a book.

The last time my spirit left my body, I was suddenly helpless and totally inactive. The muscles tightened in my throat until I couldn't talk. Weakness kept me in bed at least twenty hours a day. Losing my balance and falling happened frequently.

After the symptoms lingered for months, I was losing hope that I would ever be self-reliant. Someone had to fix my meals and drive me everywhere I went. Unexpected jerks and twitches interfered with everything I did. My voice was slurred and filled with hesitation. That hesitation also affected my thoughts. It took me a minute to even think of the names of my grandchildren. Talking on the telephone or texting was so difficult, I didn't even attempt it.

After teaching school for thirty years, I was ready to retire. I just didn't want to leave in the middle of a school year. That was hard on the students. If it had been a possibility, I would have finished the year out. I couldn't do any of the work I loved. There was not anything I could do to help my class.

Watching television got old quick! Boredom led me to the computer. Nothing I did was productive. I hated wasting time.

Daily physical therapy at the hospital strengthened my

muscles and agility. I had some weird symptoms. I could run, but I couldn't walk a straight line. I could sing, but I couldn't carry on a conversation. It was hard to sit still and focus on anything. At the computer, reading was easy. It was a real challenge to have a thought and write it down.

That's how my book began. I started writing sentences as therapy. At first, it was a struggle to write even a few short words. I made myself write my thoughts every day. After months of writing, it got easier. I decided to write about my life. Precious memories of my children and husband were the subject of my text.

Later my subject changed. I realized I had only one story to tell. That story concerns the celestial energy I encountered. It's the only thing that makes me different from other people.

At first I hesitated. *Should I share this with the world, when I could not even share it with the people I loved! It will hurt my family! People will think I am crazy! I will have to relive it!* I've never even wanted to think about these experiences.

Lately I have come to terms with what has happened to me. I can truly say I am at peace. Only now do I see the whole picture. I know I have received closure. Only now can I write these words.

I know this is not the only therapy that helped me heal. The more I wrote, the better I became. After three years, I am well enough to take care of myself. My condition doesn't keep me from doing most of the things I love.

I believe there is a purpose for this book. I know it will deliver the right message to the people who need to hear it.

Now I realize particular words were communicated to me. It was as if words were condensed to the exact message I needed to hear. Some messages came during the actual experiences. Other happened while I was writing the book.

Just a few words, so simple, but very powerful. My life was changed by the message they brought. The messengers delivered so much more than words. They imparted peace, wisdom, hope, and strength when I needed it the most.

The concept of these messages have been delivered in many stories and verses. I did not hear the concept. I heard the exact words, as if someone was talking to me.

(1) "Forgive him"
These words were repeated in my head. They were the shield that defended me from hatred. That hatred could have been Harvey's destruction.

(2) "Believe in yourself!"
The Indian angel delivered this message, along with strength and peace.

(3) "Do not fear death!"
Each time I faced death, an angel was with me.

(4) "Prayers are answered."
I witnessed the power of prayer in Cortney's recovery.

(5) "Inside each of us there is good and evil."
Although most messages came from verses in the Bible, one came from social media. I read the post of a Cherokee Indian proverb. I thought it taught a good lesson. Only years later, when I was writing my book, did I see how this proverb described our human spirit. I could not get it out of my head.

(6) "Celestial."

I was at the Huntsville Redstone Space Center watching a film about our universe when this word came to me. A star or a planet is only a speck of dust in our infinite physical world. Our spiritual world is also an infinite celestial place. Although seeing our universe on an Imax screen is very impressive, I had a more impressive experience during the film.

My senses sharpened. Visions of a spiritual world popped in my head. They were memories of places I saw when I was a spirit. This flashback is my most recent spiritual activity.

The fact that I have had angels intercede for me is not unusual. Angels are all around us, answering prayers and doing God's will. I have seen them and felt their power. If angels were there for me, they are also there for you. There's nothing special about me that deserves a guardian angel.

Even though heaven is their home, God and the angels are also on earth.

Life on earth is not all there is. We are so much more than our earthly bodies. We have God's light in us.

ABOUT THE AUTHOR

*B*etty Compton lives in a small town in Northeast Mississippi near Pickwick Lake. There she enjoys retirement. She spends much of her time in Germantown, Tennessee attending activities with her grandchildren. Betty is an avid sponsor of children's theatre and the historical society. A student of genealogy, she is the author of several accounts of early settlement in Tishomingo County, Mississippi.

Printed in the United States
By Bookmasters